PRAGUE

MANCHESTER
UNIVERSITY PRESS

The Buildings of Europe

Series adviser: Christopher Woodward

Already published

Berlin, Derek Fraser
Copenhagen, Christopher Woodward
Rome, Christopher Woodward

Forthcoming titles

Hanseatic Cities, Christoph Grafe

The Buildings of Europe

PRAGUE

Jane Pavitt

Manchester University Press

Manchester and New York

Distributed exclusively in the USA by St. Martin's Press

Published by Manchester University Press
Oxford Road, Manchester M13 9NR, UK
and
Room 400, 175 Fifth Avenue, New York,
NY 10010, USA
http://www.man.ac.uk/mup

Distributed exclusively in the USA by
St. Martin's Press, Inc., 175 Fifth Avenue, New York,
NY 10010, USA

Distributed exclusively in Canada by
UBC Press, University of British Columbia,
6344 Memorial Road, Vancouver, BC, Canada V6T 1Z2

British Library Cataloguing-in-Publication Data
A catalogue record for this book is available from the
British Library

Library of Congress Cataloging-in-Publication Data
applied for

ISBN 0 7190 3915 0 *hardback*
ISBN 0 7190 3916 9 *paperback*

First published 2000

07 06 05 04 03 02 01 00
10 9 8 7 6 5 4 3 2 1

Typography by Nick Loat

Layout by Christopher Woodward

Printed in Great Britain by
Bookcraft (Bath) Ltd,
Midsomer Norton

How to use this guide

There are 187 entries in this guide: individual buildings, housing estates, city planning projects and other historical landmarks. The entries are arranged chronologically, and divided into eight sections. The reference number of each entry also relates to its location on the maps in the back of the book. It is also advisable to acquire a detailed city map on arrival in Prague. City maps are published by Kartographie Praha and are readily available from bookshops and stands across the city. Prague's network of buses, trams and underground trains is highly efficient and inexpensive; nearly all of the sites listed are accessible by public transport. The standard city maps show the public transport routes. The Prague metro is usually the quickest way to travel but trams and buses will take you along more scenic routes. Where appropriate the nearest metro station, M, bus, B, or tram, T, service is given for each entry.

Many of the buildings are open to the public, but opening times are subject to change and so have not been listed in this guide. There are plenty of English-language tourist guides available that give general information on opening times. A number of suburban buildings, particularly modern villas, are set in private gardens that can sometimes obscure the view from the road, particularly in the height of summer. The building entry will mention if this is a difficulty.

The inclusion of a building in this guide does not mean that its grounds or interior are accessible to the public. Please respect the privacy of those living or working in the buildings listed.

Contents

Old Town Hall 7: the Clock

Introduction

The city teems with wonders; but what belongs where?
Patrick Leigh Fermor, *A Time of Gifts* (1989)

The population of Prague is approximately 1,200,000 – about an eighth of the whole population of the Czech Republic. The city occupies in the region of 500 square kilometres along the Vltava River, at a point further west than any other capital of 'eastern' Europe. The city centre is made up of five quarters: Hradčany (the Castle quarter) and Malá Strana (the Lesser Town) on the left bank; Staré Město (the Old Town), Nové Město (the New Town) and Josefov (The Old Jewish Quarter) on the right bank. To the south of the city centre is the district of Vyšehrad (meaning 'high castle'). This guide deals largely with selected buildings in these quarters, but also includes a significant number of buildings from the suburbs and the outlying districts. They have been selected to chart the cultural, social and economic history of the city, as well as for their architectural significance.

The shaping of the city

The Vltava River in Bohemia flows mostly through deep valleys and gorges. At the point in the river where the city now stands is a terrace, or sill, which made fording possible. The origin of the Czech name Praha is still debated, but it is possible it meant this little outcrop, or, alternatively, 'a household threshold' (*prah*). The hilly region around this point in the Vltava valley has been inhabited since neolithic times. The city itself grew up from the eighth century with the settlement of Slavonic tribes. According to legend, the Slav princess Libuše had prophesied the founding of a great city on this site; her own marriage to a ploughman, Přemysl, established the Přemyslid dynasty, which was to rule Bohemia for six centuries. Whatever the origins of the city, Prague developed as a lively centre through which merchants and traders from the east and west would pass.

Introduction

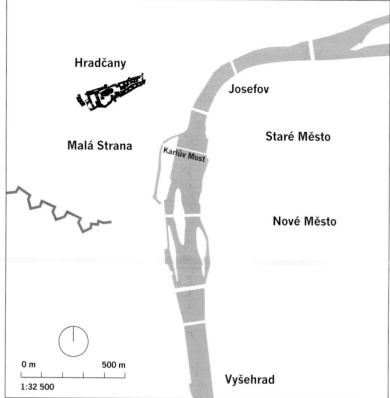

Prague's quarters

The cluster of settlements which grew up on both the left and right bank of the Vltava on the site of what was to become Prague was dominated by three fortified castle sites: Hradčany (the seat of the Přemyslid dynasty) 1, Vyšehrad (to the south) 2 and Levý Hradec (to the north). By the early tenth century the settlement at Levý Hradec had been superseded by the more powerful Hradčany. At about this time the castle site at Vyšehrad was established. Vyšehrad was traditionally held to be the first seat of Přemyslid power, and hence has long been associated with the birth of Czech nationhood. However, archaeological findings have shown Vyšehrad to be a later fortified site than was originally thought.

The city's importance grew from its religious status and its place on European trade routes. In 973, after a period of religious difficulty, Prague received its charter from Rome to found the first Bishopric. The first Bohemian monastery was established at Hradčany, and this began a grand tradition of religious architecture in the city. As well as this, early development included a mercantile quarter on the right bank of the river, the centre of which is now the Old Town

Square. The route from the castle to the market was connected by the main river crossing at Judith's Bridge, replaced by the Charles Bridge 11 in 1357.

Bohemia's independent rule was brought to an end in 1620 at the infamous Battle of the White Mountain. In the intervening period, Prague's architectural character was determined by the following factors: royal and civic patronage, the founding of religious communities in the city and the growth of mercantile wealth. By the thirteenth century, Prague was fast becoming a centre of European significance, attracting German and Jewish merchants and craftsmen. The most dense areas of development outside the castle walls were the Old Town and neighbouring Jewish ghetto. In 1212, Bohemia was granted a hereditary kingship by the emperor, Frederick II. In 1257, under Otakar II, the region of Malá Strana (the Lesser Town) was laid out below the castle to accommodate the new settlers. The city's intellectual heritage benefited from the founding of the Charles University 10 in 1348.

The physical evidence of the city's early history can be found all over Prague. The medieval street plan may have been obliterated in some later phases of redevelopment, but the alleys and passageways in the areas closest to the Charles Bridge and around the Old Town Square map out ancient routes. Baroque street façades often conceal earlier buildings, and the forms of Romanesque dwellings can be seen in courtyards and building basements. The sites of monasteries and convents are perhaps the best indication of this period's innovations in terms of artistic patronage and building technology.

View of Hradčany and Malá Strana

Introduction

Charles IV's golden city

Prague's 'golden age' was to come with the arrival of Charles IV (1316–78) after he was made governor of Bohemia and Moravia in 1333. Despite his itinerant life abroad, Prague was Charles' spiritual home. However, he found a city quite dilapidated and Prague Castle almost destroyed after several years of decline. Charles embarked on a major reconstruction and town planning programme, rebuilding the castle and creating several magnificent architectural projects in the city, such as the bridge which now bears his name. On the site of the old Rotunda of St Vitus in the castle, which had been established by Wenceslas in 925, Charles ordered the building of a grand Gothic Cathedral. In 1348, the city expanded with the planning of Nové Město (the New Town) on the east side of the river, adjacent to the Old Town. In the same year, Charles established the first Central European University, later called the Carolinum, or Charles University. The town's fortifications, completed by 1350, stretched around the Hradčany and the Lesser Town, and, on the opposite side of the river, around the New Town reaching as far as Vyšehrad.

Charles' political power extended far beyond Bohemia, but he chose to make Prague his centre of cultural, intellectual and economic activity. In 1355, when he was made Holy Roman Emperor, Prague was named as the imperial capital. By the end of his reign the city was one of the largest and most prosperous in Europe, with a population of almost 50,000.

Religious struggle and the Bohemian renaissance

The increased power and wealth given to the Catholic church during Charles' reign was to fuel the religious and political crisis that troubled the city after his death. The call for religious reform, which had its origins in England with John Wycliffe, was taken up in Prague by Jan Hus, the dean of philosophy at Charles University. Hus also contributed to the spread of a Czech nationalist struggle, urging Bohemia to turn its back on German cultural domination and create a new Czech identity. In 1415, Hus was burned at the stake as a heretic and his followers began an uprising, demanding both religious reform and the foundation of an independent Czech national state. The Hussite Wars raged across Central Europe from 1419–35. By the end of that period, few Hussite demands had been realised, but a tradition of national aspiration and identity was established.

In the more peaceful years that followed, building work was renewed and the city rewarded with many Late Gothic projects. In 1471, the Polish Jagiellon dynasty came to power in Prague, and Vladislav II continued the tradition of artistic patronage and architectural activity in the city. The work of Benedikt Ried, the architect of the great Vladislav Hall in the castle, created a fusion of late Gothic style and early Renaissance influence. By the early sixteenth century, émigré artists and architects were arriving from Italy and Germany, and a new, largely secular architecture developed. Ferdinand I invited Italian builders to redesign the castle gardens and build a summer palace, the Belvedere 19, based on a Palladian model. In 1541, a great fire swept through the Lesser Town, prompting a period of rebuilding.

The end of the sixteenth century was marked by a second 'golden age', and the triumph of late Renaissance art (sometimes called Rudolfian Mannerism) under the patronage of Rudolf II (1576–1612) who made Prague once again the capital of the Holy Roman Empire in 1584. Architects combined the principles of Italian Mannerism with vernacular detail and decoration such as sgraffito to create a specifically Bohemian Renaissance style. Rudolf also gathered astronomers, physicians and scientists to his court, including the English alchemists, John Dee and Edward Kelley.

This surge of cultural activity was marred by increasing political unrest between the Bohemian Protestant nobles and the imperial aristocracy. Rudolf's brother, Matthias, was made king of Bohemia in 1612, but the title of emperor had been revoked and Prague ceased to be the capital of empire. During his short reign, Matthias was deeply affected by religious troubles, as was his successor, Ferdinand II. In 1618, Protestant nobles threw two imperial representatives (and a secretary) from the windows of Prague Castle as a protest against the choice of Frederick II as the new Bohemian ruler. They all landed safely on a dungheap, but the act prompted riots in the city. The League of Catholics responded with a show of military aggression. On 8 November 1620, the Protestant Estates Union was defeated at the Battle of the White Mountain (Bílá Hora) and Bohemia became subject to Hapsburg rule.

Baroque Prague

At the outset of the Thirty Years War, the Protestant Union in Prague was defeated and its landed members forced into exile. Following further conflict with domestic and foreign powers, the re-Catholicisation of Bohemia and Moravia began in earnest. Prague never regained its status as the centre of Holy Roman Empire, and any idea of a national, Protestant consciousness was suppressed. As the independent power of the Czech lands diminished, the city entered a period of decline. The castle lost its status as the seat of monarchy and government,

Introduction

The Loreto 40 : detail

estates were confiscated and homes deserted, lowering the value of property in the city. Although the wars had left their mark on Prague, a new wave of building was about to begin. In the two centuries after the Peace of Westphalia in 1648, which confirmed the removal of Prague's sovereign status, the city developed as the built expression of Catholic Hapsburg domination. The growth of a strong Hapsburg power and the steady rise of the Baroque went hand in hand.

In 1648, Prague was occupied briefly by the Swedish armies. The Hapsburg response was to organise the fortification of the city once again, reinforcing the remaining Gothic town walls, and adding eleven grand gateways. The complex fortifications were the work of Hapsburg military engineers and foreign architects, such as Carlo Lurago, who settled in Prague. Inside the new walls, the city continued to enjoy an unprecedented wave of building. Catholic nobles, eager to seize the chance of acquiring land and position, vied with each other to build grand palaces and estates. The palaces of Wallenstein 23, Černin 26 and Clam-Gallas 35 are testament to this enormous civil wealth. The Catholic church also built many of its greatest monuments during the same period. Towards the end of the seventeenth century, much of the middle-class housing was renewed (often town houses built on an older set of foundations) and many medieval churches rebuilt.

The possibilities of such wealthy patronage attracted architects and artisans from other parts of Europe, namely France, Italy and Bavaria. These included the Dientzenhofer family, Carlo and Anselmo Lurago, Domenico Orsi, Jean-Baptiste

Mathey, Giovanni Battista Alliprandi and the lesser known Johann Santini-Aichl. The Italian connection was also the result of Austria's close links following the Treaty of Utrecht. Bohemian Baroque developed its own specific character, which tended to distinguish it from the rest of Europe. In stylistic terms, this is exemplified in the work of the younger Dientzenhofer, Kilian Ignaz, who developed a rather joyous and dynamic Baroque style. In the first phase of Baroque development, characterised by the refortification of the city, huge sections of the city were razed to make way for new buildings. By the end of the seventeenth century, this practice was replaced by a more sensitive approach to the planning of the city. Many Baroque buildings retained their Gothic core – it is often an architecture of façadism, wrapped around the existing fabric of the city. Architects such as Dientzenhofer instigated a shift away from the massive regularity of Italian Baroque, towards a more curvaceous style. The Prague-born Italian architect, Giovanni Santini-Aichl, a contemporary of Kilian Ignaz Dientzenhofer, combined the Baroque with a use of Gothic historicism.

If the first phase of architectural development in this period shows the arrogance of newly acquired power, this second phase has the hallmarks of a culture at ease with itself, consolidating its successes by the outward display of splendid wealth and artistic riches. By the mid eighteenth century, the number of large-scale commissions was considerably fewer, and there was a shift towards a more decorative and less dramatic architectural language, showing some inspiration from French Rococo. The patron, Count Franz Anton Sporck, favoured Viennese-influenced architects like Giovanni Battista Alliprandi, a native of Prague, who also designed the Lobkowicz Palace **33**. The Viennese court architect Nicholas Pacassi remodelled Prague Castle in a style that marked the return of a more regular and severe Neo-classicism. Another architect from the Viennese Court, Johann Bernhard Fischer von Erlach, designed the Clam-Gallas Palace **35** in 1715.

The line of Hapsburg emperors continued to rule Bohemia as part of the Holy Roman Empire, successfully staving off challenges to their control throughout the eighteenth century. When Maria Theresa inherited the imperial title, her claim was challenged in the War of Austrian Succession, during which time Prague was occupied for two years. Several years later, the city was besieged again during the Seven Years War. The city sustained much damage during this period, and Maria Theresa instigated a building programme which included Pacassi's remodelling of the castle. Maria Theresa's son, Josef II, began a policy of reform for the city, which included the abolition of serfdom in 1781, and his 'Edict of Toleration' the following year. This allowed greater freedom of movement among

Introduction

Czech and German people, precipitating a rise in patriotic Czech feeling, and the development of an enlightened, secular intelligentsia.

Prague flourished in this new atmosphere of tolerance, attracting new business and industry, and rapidly increasing its population. Alongside this, the establishment of academic institutions and arts societies fuelled the growing awareness of Czech national consciousness. In 1784, Josef created a single administration for the four towns that comprised Prague, an act which contributed to the gradual emancipation of the Czech lands, giving them a more powerful capital. However, this change did not halt the 'Germanisation' of both culture and state administration, which was common to all Hapsburg lands.

Industry and reform

The abolition of serfdom in 1781 had attracted a new population to Prague, which included those seeking refuge from the Napoleonic wars in Europe. Between 1800 and 1850, Prague's population almost doubled. This demographic shift, coupled with Prague's industrial expansion, had a significant effect upon attitudes to the Hapsburg empire. Tensions between the imperial power and the Czech community were apparent, as the new Czech middle classes objected to the Hapsburgian insistence upon the primacy of German language and culture. In Prague, a number of learned societies promoted the use of the Czech language. This aided the development of a strong national movement, under the leadership of historian František Palacký. The revolutionary events of 1848 in Europe were marked by a Czech uprising in Prague, which was violently suppressed by imperial troops. However, the granting of certain concessions followed, including giving Prague the right of self-administration in 1860. Although the imperial cultural and political influence in Prague was declining, when Austria conceded to nationalist demands from Hungary, forming the Austro-Hungarian alliance in 1866, Bohemia's demands were ignored.

In architectural terms, the first few decades of the nineteenth century have often been dismissed as a period of 'inertia', when a drab and uniform 'Empire style' characterised much public building in Bohemia. This view ignores the crucial innovations of the period, which had a profound effect upon the urban fabric of Prague. The new wealth generated by successful industry contributed to the rise of a new urban Czech population. In Prague, new suburbs grew up around centres of manufacturing, including Karlín 48, Smíchov, Libeň and Holešovice. Architectural activity had been affected by the introduction of building regulations since 1780, and then progressively by the growth of technical expertise and new materials. The arrival of the railways at Prague in 1845 had a significant effect. The development of Prague's manufacturing base meant that this was also a period of new constructional achievements and a time when the building trades benefited from the influx of craftsmen and engineers. Changes in the social structure of the city meant the need for new building types: factories, new forms of housing, and social and military institutions. After 1817, new town planning regulations authorised the construction of new suburbs, of which Karlín was the first.

By the middle of the century, a sense of Czech historical and folk identity was apparent in the visual arts, literature and music. Prague was transformed by this wave of artistic and political activity. The Czech Academy of Sciences and Arts was founded in 1890, a few years after Charles University established a Czech-language division. Artists and architects found national expression through the revival of past styles. By the 1870s, the dominant trend in this new eclecticism was the revival of Renaissance models, pioneered by architects Josef Zítek and Josef Schulz. This movement also championed the need for a closer relationship between architecture and crafts. Undoubtedly, the English Gothic Revival and the work of French architect Eugène Viollet-de-Duc were key influences, specifically on the drive to 'restore' many medieval buildings. From 1850, the state supported the conservation and renovation of historic buildings in the city, although national romanticism encouraged architects in a sometimes misguided reinvention of past styles on historic buildings.

Vyšehrad Cemetery 57

Introduction

As architects sought to establish a so-called 'national style', a number of important historicist monuments (such as the National Theatre 58 and the National Museum 59) were built. One of the most significant national events of the late nineteenth century was the Jubilee Exhibition 64 of 1891, which celebrated 100 years of scientific, artistic and industrial achievement. This was followed four years later by the Czechoslovak Ethnographic Exhibition. The Ethnographic exhibition precipitated the Folk movement, and a greater interest in ethnicity. The use of the vernacular in architecture, however, was not considered by its advocates as simply another form of revivalism. Instead, they regarded the vernacular as indicative of an indigenous living culture. Architects were interested in the construction of traditional wooden architecture, and what they saw as its inherent 'truthfulness'. Of course, the impact of the English Arts and Crafts movement had partly inspired this development, and architects borrowed from English domestic architecture in their search for a freely planned and functional villa type.

Despite the use of historicist and vernacular styles, the Jubilee Exhibition had also given architects and engineers the opportunity to deploy new constructional techniques such as those seen in Paris at the Expositions. Architects also looked to Paris and Vienna as planning models for the redevelopment of the city. On the edges of the Old Town, the old Jewish ghetto was prepared for demolition and the redevelopment of a new quarter for the new urban bourgeoisie.

Jewish Prague

The Jewish community had existed for ten centuries or more, since the first Jewish settlers arrived and the ghetto was established in the tenth century. The ghetto grew up in the vicinity of what is now Josefov 63, with the Old–New Synagogue 6 as its spiritual and physical centre. Alternately favoured or persecuted by successive rulers, the Jewish community was granted certain privileges that influenced the growth of this area of the city. In 1410, the Jewish cemetery and its immediate vicinity was protected by decree.

The original ghetto, once referred to as V Židech or 'in the Jews', was separated from the Christian Communities by seven gatehouses. The ghetto suffered intermittent ransackings during periods of turmoil in the city, usually by militant mobs who would use disorder as an excuse to pillage Jewish homes. During the seventeenth and eighteenth centuries, the boundaries of the ghetto gradually extended, with Jewish merchants buying property outside of the original gates. As more refugees and new settlers came to the city, the ghetto became hopelessly overcrowded. In 1689, after a plague epidemic throughout the whole city,

Jewish cemetery

the wooden buildings of the ghetto were destroyed in a fire, which also damaged parts of the Old and New Towns. The ghetto was rebuilt relatively quickly, but many Jews left to settle in other parts of the city. In the early nineteenth century the walls of the ghetto were removed, and in 1848 Jewish citizens were granted equal rights. Two years later the old ghetto was acknowledged as the fifth sector of the city, and given the name Josefov. This was followed by a period of increasing self awareness and intellectual freedom for the Jewish community, marked by the growth of the Czech–Jewish movement.

The old ghetto, still a crowded confusion of buildings, became dominated by the poor, who could not afford to leave. Only the most orthodox stayed for religious reasons. By 1890, only about a fifth of the population of Josefov was Jewish. Overcrowding, lack of maintenance and inadequate sewers meant that it had become a squalid area. The writer Gustav Meyrink characterised the Prague ghetto in his 1915 novel, *Golem*, as 'a demonic underworld, a place of anguish, a beggarly and phantasmic quarter ... An expression of the weakened state of Europe at the beginning of the new century. ' By the new century, however, the old ghetto had almost entirely disappeared. In 1885, a proposal for slum clearance was put forward for Josefov and selected areas of the Old and New Towns. A plan was selected, and clearance began in 1893. Only the town hall, the cemetery and six synagogues were left, and a new fashionable quarter, with its main access connecting the old town with a (new) bridge over the river, was built.

Introduction

The path to nationhood

The idealism of the Czech patriotic movement was given a new impetus by the rise to prominence in the 1890s of Tomáš Masaryk, a young professor at the Charles University. Masaryk argued for a progressive approach to national identity, rather than an aggressive nationalism. He proposed union with Slovakia, once it was freed from Hungarian control. Masaryk's approach aptly coincides with the shift among the Prague artistic community away from historicism. A younger generation of artists and architects responded to Masaryk's ambitions. His plea for a progressive Czech movement reinforced their rejection of a historicising culture in favour of an emergent modernism. This generation looked to avant-garde developments in the rest of Europe. Prague's economic boom and corresponding expansion provided work for a new generation of architects who sought to express the nature of modernity through their buildings. Art Nouveau and Secessionist styles were deployed in the decoration of many private residences and commercial developments.

Historicism was gradually superseded between 1900–10 by the use of Art Nouveau and Secessionist styles (although many buildings of the pre-war period happily combine the two). The use of Nature in both constructive and decorative elements was found to be a suitable alternative to the use of past styles. Naturalistic and Symbolist languages were imbued with a spiritual sense that implied rebirth and regeneration. Architects worked closely with painters and sculptors,

Art Nouveau detail

18

creating a closely knit avant-garde community in Prague, which was encouraged by commercial and private patrons, who commissioned new villas and stores as well as speculative residential and commercial development.

The generation of architects from the 1880s and 1890s, led by Antonín Wiehl and Josef Fanta represented the transitional phases between historicism and the modern, and gave Prague some of its greatest late-nineteenth-century buildings. Of course, the important link between Prague and Vienna continued, and many young Czech architects trained under Secessionist architects, Joseph Olbrich and Otto Wagner. Unquestionably, the most important figure to come from this direction was Jan Kotěra, known as the 'father' of modern Czech architecture. A comparison of Kotěra's Trmal Villa of 1902 (Vilová 11, Strašnice) with his own family villa in Vinohrady of 1908 **91**, shows how the modern villa type developed out of an exploration of traditional vernacular architecture.

In 1898, Kotěra returned to Prague from Vienna to be appointed professor of the school of applied arts. Kotěra had worked with Otto Wagner in Vienna, and his work (and that of his students) signalled a shift towards this more rational and synthetic design. Kotěra's advocacy of architectural 'honesty' and humble materials and his views on the regulation of ornament indicate his influences, from C. F. A. Voysey and C. R. Mackintosh to Louis Sullivan and Frank Lloyd Wright. He travelled considerably, absorbing the lessons of Berlage in Holland

Villa Trmal, 1902

Introduction

Otto Gutfreund, *The Motorcyclist*

and the English Garden City Movement. His work was also governed by a sense of social responsibility. Kotěra more than any other single figure orchestrated the break with the past, and he was the presiding influence over the next generation of architects.

This new generation, including architects such as Pavel Janák and Josef Gočar, developed a less rational and more spiritual and subjective approach. Despite Kotěra's influence, they argued increasingly for an architecture where (in Janák's words) 'artistic thought and abstraction will take over leadership from practicality'. Borrowing from the fine arts, they developed an architectural vocabulary known as 'Czech Cubism'.

Czech Cubism

The impact that Czech Cubism had on Prague's architecture and design has been exhaustively reassessed in the last few years. The influence of French painting, the deconstruction of matter and the exploration of the space surrounding objects in the work of Picasso, Braque and others, influenced the development of this idiosyncratic and unique artistic movement. However, Czech Cubism was not just simply the application of these principles to architecture. In his essay, 'The Prism and the Pyramid' (1912), Pavel Janák argued that cubistic and pyramidal forms were the manifestation of the artist's own subjectivity, as well as the expression of a set of abstract, universal laws. For Janák in particular, the pyramidal cubist forms he utilised represented the transcendence of the human spirit. According to Janák, if Kotěra's rectangular masses represented the material, utilitarian world, then the exploded fractured forms of Cubism meant dynamism and transformation. These ideas were applied to the furniture and interiors, ceramics, glass and textiles, a number of temporary exhibition pavilions and a host of unrealised projects. The key remaining Cubist buildings are listed in this guide; the applied arts can be found in collections of the Museum of Decorative Arts. The style was also argued to have a close affinity with the Baroque character of the city, although it was by no means revivalist. Architects Janák, Gočar, Josef Chochol and Vlastislav Hofman joined with artists Emil Filla, Otto Gutfreund and Bohumil Kubišta to promote the new art through the *Skupina výtvarných umělců* (The Society of Creative Artists), founded in 1911. After the end of World War I, some Cubist architects, such as Janák and Gočar, attempted to reinvent Cubism as a 'national style', combining with it references

Diamant House 108, detail

Introduction

to traditional wooden architecture and using colour to evoke the national flag. National Style, or 'Rondo-Cubism' as it became known because of the addition of semi-circular forms to the vocabulary of geometric decoration, only lasted a few years. Rounded forms and painted decoration were applied to the façades of buildings, as well as to the applied arts produced by the arts and crafts co-operatives, *Artěl*, and the Prague Art Workshops, *Pražské umělecké dílny*. Josef Chochol and Vlastislav Hofman argued against this, in favour of a form of Cubism with 'mathematical precision', much closer to the Purism of Jeanneret (Le Corbusier) and Amédée Ozenfant in Paris. By the mid 1920s, after the building of the monumental Adria Palace 115, Janák had renounced this direction, turning to what he saw as the more fundamental development of Functionalism. Many of the protagonists of Czech Cubism were active in the growth of the Czech Modern Movement after the war.

Between the wars: the new Czechoslovak state

During the war, Masaryk had led the struggle for Czech independence from a position of exile, travelling around Europe and finally founding the Czechoslovak National Council in Paris in 1918, together with Edvard Beneš. Masaryk's political manoeuvres in Europe and the USA were given further support by the founding of the Czech Legion in 1917, a division which fought alongside the Allies against Germany and Austro-Hungary. Masaryk reached agreement with the Slovaks over their proposed union in May 1918 at talks held in the USA. On 28 October 1918, after their return to Prague, the provisional government declared the founding of the Czechoslovak Republic, with Masaryk elected soon after as its president.

The period of modern architecture in Czechoslovakia from 1918–38 has been afforded considerable attention by architectural historians. In Prague, the level of intellectual debate and contact with other European nations, via the international-ism of the Modern Movement, all contributed to one of the most creative and progressive periods in the arts. A number of different directions developed. The creation of the new republic in 1918, with Prague as its capital, prompted much debate on the future of the historic city, already under pressure from rapid expansion. President Masaryk, moving offices to Prague Castle, ordered renova-tion and rebuilding work which was largely carried out by Josip Plečnik 120. New ministries, governmental and administrative buildings were needed, and public competitions were organised to produce a suitable architecture that would meet with state approval. In 1919, the State Planning Commission was established, in order to formulate a set of planning regulations for the city and its environs, brought together by the Greater Prague Act of 1921. Public competitions were held and architects invited to produce planning solutions for designated areas of the city, such as Letná Plain and Dejvice 118. Legislation was brought in to try to protect the historic core of the city and prevent ad hoc development.

A polemical and politicised avant-garde came out of the architecture schools in the early 1920s. The development of Functionalism, rather than the attempts by Janák to create a fusion of Cubism with Folk style, offered potential to those in search of an appropriate modern language. The traditionalism of some architectural teaching was criticised by a group of disaffected students, Karel Honzík, Evžen Linhart, Vít Obrtel and Jaroslav Fragner, known as *Puristicka čtyřka* (The Purist Four). Purism advocated a simplified, harmonious language of architecture and was swiftly developed by Gočar, Chochol and a host of younger architects, who also looked to the purism and *l'esprit nouveau* of Le Corbusier in Paris.

Marxism, Russian Constructivism, and the anticipation of 'a new social organisation of life' dictated the development of Czech Functionalism in the later 1920s. After some initial unease with the social implications of modern technology, the avant garde *Devĕstil* group of artists, writers, filmmakers and designers adopted this approach, celebrating the products of modern life. The work of Jaromír Krejcar typified this attitude. Functionalism essentially developed in two directions: scientific functionalism (which regarded architecture primarily as a technical tool) and emotional functionalism (which argued for the psychological and aesthetic importance of architecture). The two factions maintained a vigorous debate throughout the period.

Housing reform was a central consideration. In the later 1920s, a number of communities were planned for the lower working classes. Several of these used a garden city model, but increasingly architects on the left became interested in the design of multi-storey and communal apartment blocks. Such projects were published and discussed in the avant-garde journals of the day – particularly *Stavba*, edited by the *Devĕstil* spokesman, Karel Teige. The extreme leftist factions within the avant garde – namely the groups *Levá Fronta*, ARDEV (part of *Devĕstil*) and PAS (*Pracovní architektonická skupina* or the Architectural Working Group) – developed a range of planning solutions that influenced the development of a Czech socialist architecture immediately after World War II.

The dominance of Functionalism in the 1930s not only resulted in the planning of large-scale public housing projects, but also a large number of open-plan, white-walled and flat-roofed Modernist villas. These middle-class homes, greatly

Introduction

influenced by Le Corbusier, Mies Van der Rohe and Adolf Loos, became the hallmark of Czech Modernism between the wars. Le Corbusier's visits to Prague in the 1920s and 1930s never resulted in any commissions, although he contributed to the urban projects of the Bat'a company in Zlín in the 1930s. Mies and Loos 145, however, both built villas in Czechoslovakia, which are among the most celebrated European examples of the period. Mies's Tugendhat house in Brno, although not listed in this book, deserves mentioning; it is not an isolated example as Brno has a wealth of Modernist buildings from the interwar period. Patronised by a wealthy bourgeoisie, the abundance of private housing built in the period shows the interest in Modernist forms and interior planning, while retaining traditional notions of family living and social organisation. There are a large number of striking examples of villa architecture in Prague and its environs, many of them built for the intelligentsia or the artistic elite, such as the Villa Frič (Na lysinách 15/208, Hodkovičky), designed by Ladislav Žak in 1934–35 for the film director Martin Frič. Often located in out-of-the-way sites, amid mature landscaping and built on hillsides for the views, many of these private homes (like the Villa Frič) are inaccessible and invisible to the passing visitor. Some of the more accessible are included in this guide.

Both in the centre of the city and in the expanding suburbs, Functionalism was employed to create new department stores, hotels, bars and civic and commercial buildings. For several leading Czech companies the employment of avant-garde architects gave them an image of being both modern and international. Again, the Bat'a Shoe company of Zlín is a good example of such patronage. Bat'a employed young modern architects from all over Czechoslovakia to design department stores and contribute to the development of their factory towns both at home and abroad 141. At the International Exhibitions of the 1920s and 1930s, the Czechoslovak nation presented a forthright Modernist image to complement their image as an expanding and industrialising young European nation.

The economic crisis of the 1930s, precipitated by the 1929 Wall Street Crash, had a disastrous effect on the building industry. Government-subsidised worker housing complexes kept some in employment, and architects developed high-density, low-cost solutions in response to architectural competitions. Modernist architects engaged with radical left-wing politics, organising societies and publishing polemical texts and projects. A number of built projects in the 1930s show how architects strove to create significant new building types, as witness Gillar's French Schools 151 and Linhart's Secondary School 157 in Dejvice, and Havlíček and Honzík's General Pension Institute 147. By the end of the 1930s, there was a tendency towards a more restrained Functionalism with Neo-classical overtones (in the work of Jaroslav Fragner), but this period of creativity and experimentation was drawing rapidly to a close.

World War II

The freedom the young nation had experienced during the 1920s and 1930s was interrupted as the political situation in Europe worsened. In 1938, the Sudeten German Party, on Hitler's instructions, formally asked the Czech government for more rights than they knew the Czechs would be prepared to grant, including incorporation of the German–Czech regions into the German Reich. The government refused, but the Allies pressed for cooperation in an attempt to avoid a wider European confrontation. Masaryk's successor, President Edvard Beneš, resigned and fled to London. Just as German troops marched into the Sudeten territories, the Slovaks declared themselves an autonomous state within the Czechoslovak Republic. A shaky peace seemed to have been established, despite the division of the nation, but only until Hitler's further plans for Czechoslovakia became clear. In 1939, under the threat of the German military, the Czech president, Emil Hácha, signed an agreement in Berlin that established the Reich Protectorate of Bohemia and Moravia. The region was developed as a centre for Nazi industrial and military manufacture, and any resistance resulted in the closing of universities and the deportation or internment of detractors.

In exile, Beneš established a provisional government with the support of the Allies and the aid of the Soviet Union. The Nazi occupation of Prague resulted in the deaths of a vast proportion of the Jewish population, most of them sent to Auschwitz or the infamous 'model' concentration camp at Terezin. After the withdrawal of German troops several days before the end of the war, an uprising in Prague resulted in the expelling of German civilians, just as Soviet Liberation troops marched into the city.

From annexation to independence

Beneš returned to Prague in 1945 and established a new government which set about the nationalisation of industry. In 1946, the Czech Communist Party was voted into power, with Klement Gottwald as prime minister. After a coup in 1948, the Communist Party seized total control, expelled all non-communists from government posts and rigged the next election. Beneš resigned, leaving Gottwald as president. The following years saw the increasing Sovietisation of Czech politics and culture, even after the deaths of Stalin and Gottwald, until 1960 when the People's Republic of Czechoslovakia was renamed the Socialist Republic (ČSSR).

Introduction

After the Communist Party came to power in 1948, the key feature of architectural practice was the search for uniform standards and building types that would aid large-scale development. Many of these issues had been raised by those Modernists from radical, left-wing associations in the 1930s. By the 1950s, the nature of professional practice had changed as well, as the state became the main client of architects. In the early 1950s, Czech architecture came under the influence of Socialist Realism. Between 1948 and 1956, a number of projects that attempted to create a people's socialist and historicist architecture were built in Czechoslovakia, including Jiří Kroha's temporary buildings for the 1948 Slavonic Agricultural Exhibition, and a number of housing projects in the mining region around Ostrava. Only a few projects in Prague were actually built before the 'cult of Stalin' was denounced by Kruschev in late 1954, a year after Stalin's death. The infamous Stalin monument on Letná Plain, designed in 1950 by sculptor Otakar Švec and architects Jiří and Vlasta Štursa, was torn down in 1962.

It was in the area of mass housing that the architecture of socialism had its most widespread effect. In the late 1940s and early 1950s, a number of experimental housing projects were constructed, where leftist architects tried to put into practice their pronouncements of the 1930s. The first key example of this is probably the 1946 Solidarita Housing Estate, on Černokostelecká Street in Strašnice, designed by František Jech, Karel Storch and Hanuš Majer. This was the first postwar estate to be built on a cooperative basis, and is an example of mixed development. However, such attempts at community-oriented planning were superseded by the increasing systematisation of architecture, and the application of mass standards to housing independent of individual circumstances. Huge, characterless, system-built housing estates mushroomed all over industrial areas of Czechoslovakia, and still dominate the skyline around Prague. In the 1970s, some consideration was given to community planning, with the development of Prague's 'New Towns'. The expanding suburbs were linked to the city centre by the new underground railway system, finally begun in 1965.

Other developments in the 1950s included a number of sensitive additions to the historical city, such as Jaroslav Fragner's Charles University extension 10, and his reconstruction of the Bethlehem Chapel 16. A policy of 'listing' the nation's cultural monuments began in 1962, and the city was designated a protected historic region in 1971. At Expo 58 in Brussels, Czech architects and designers presented an elegant and sophisticated late Functionalism, which can be seen in the buildings which were moved to Prague after the Expo 165. In the 1960s, Czech architects were also engaged with other architectural debates such as

Brutalism, although the most significant Czech Brutalist building was built abroad: the Czechoslovak Embassy in Notting Hill, London, by Jan Šrámek and Jan Bočan, in 1969.

In the mid 1960s, the Czech Communist Party, in an attempt to win back the loyalty of the people, implemented a series of social and civil reforms. Under the leadership of Alexander Dubček, the party offered 'socialism with a human face', and the possibility of a Communist state independent of the USSR. However, when the reform movement and the lifting of censorship rules led to the democratic uprising of 1968, the so-called 'Prague Spring', demonstrations were quickly and brutally quelled by Warsaw Pact troops. Dubček was expelled, and a tight Soviet control was imposed, which was maintained throughout the 1970s.

After the political upheaval marked by the Prague Spring in 1968, creative architectural practice was severely limited by state control and the dominance of system building and pre-fabrication for mass housing. As construction standards declined, and projects took an increasingly long time to complete, architecture appeared to stagnate. By the 1980s, however, a revitalised approach developed on the periphery of practice, with younger architects simultaneously reviving the social imperative of Functionalism, as well as looking towards postmodernism. A clearer freedom of ideas was seen in the mid to late 1980s, with projects like the *Urbanita* exhibitions (1985–90).

The velvet revolution and beyond

By the 1980s, economic difficulties and events in the rest of Communist Europe led to the rise of an increasingly vocal democratic movement. The movement was headed by the authors of the famous human rights 'Charter 77', including dissident playwright Václav Havel. Following a year of open criticism of the government, demonstrations were held in the streets of Prague in 1989. After an initial violent clash, events were generally peaceful as demonstrations spread across the country, and the civil rights groups formed themselves into a political party, Civic Forum. Under the weight of public pressure, the Communist leaders resigned and a new government was formed without any Communist majority. The public effectively demanded that Havel assume the role of president, chanting '*Havel na Hrad*' (or 'Havel to the Castle') during demonstrations.

Since the events of 1989, and following the split between the Czech and Slovak states in 1992, Prague has become a visibly more prosperous city. Foreign investment has meant a number of prestigious developments have been, or are

Introduction

Metronome, Letna Plain

in the process of being, built. This has also led to the commercially funded restoration of many buildings by companies looking for new premises or investment possibilities. After 1989, the government instituted a programme of 'restitution', through which private individuals could claim back property confiscated or 'nationalised' after the 1948 coup. This has meant some uncertainty over ownership and unstable property prices and rents. Years of neglect have also resulted in the need for expensive reconstruction, particularly of housing and services. As well as coping with these problems, the Prague authorities have to protect the historic character of the city against what might be seen as too-hurried development. Foreign investment and the rapid growth of tourism in Prague have also brought the need for new regulations relating to development and the protection of the environment. The remarkable success of Prague as both a business and tourist centre has brought many financial rewards, but the standard of living for many Czechs is still low.

The Czech architectural and design profession has diversified considerably, with many setting up small ateliers and private practices. Prague's reintegration into Europe has also attracted leading architects – such as Jean Nouvel and Frank Gehry 184 – from around the world, to participate in competitions and symposia, such as 'Workshop Prague 91', which looked into the future development of the city.

While researching this guide, many of the buildings listed have been restored or reconstructed, or have changed hands or use. I have attempted to keep track of these changes and to note their effect upon the character of the building and the city as a whole. In some cases, these changes have meant greater access to buildings of note, including the conversion of two significant modern buildings to new museums of design. In other cases, insensitive restoration has resulted in commercial pastiche. In terms of future development, it must be hoped that Prague will continue in its tradition of architectural innovation and distinctiveness, which this book aims to highlight.

Prařský Hrad (Prague Castle), 1: Mathias Gateway

The shaping of Prague c. 900–1620

1Af Pražský hrad (Prague Castle) and Cathedral of St Vitus founded c. 890

Hradčany

M Hradčanska

For 1,000 years, Prague Castle has been the centre of Czech nationhood. It has served as the home of a Bohemian monarchy and, at one time, was the seat of the Holy Roman Empire. Since 1918, it has been the political centre of the newly independent Czech state, a role that was reaffirmed in 1989. The castle was founded in about 890 by Prince Bořivoj, who made it the seat of the Přemyslid dynasty. At Levý Hradec, his previous residence, Bořivoj had created the first Christian sanctuary in Bohemia, and at the castle site in Prague he created the second. The next generation of Přemyslid princes encircled the castle with ramparts, and rebuilt it in stone. The founding of the Rotunda of St Vitus by Wenceslas I resulted in Prague being made a bishopric in 973. Further developments included the fortification of the castle by Soběslav I, parts of which still remain. These fortifications demarcated the castle area for another 500 years.

After a fire in 1303, the castle was enlarged by Charles IV. It was at this time that the castle was designated the seat of the Holy Roman Empire. The additions included the creation of one of Europe's finest Gothic cathedrals, St Vitus. However, for many years after Charles, the castle was virtually abandoned, first during the reign of Wenceslas IV, and then due to the effects of the Hussite wars.

In 1484, King Vladislav II Jagiello returned to the castle and began a number of grand reconstruction works. The tradition of princely patronage was upheld by the Jagiellion dynasty and then by Emperor Rudolf II who once again made Prague the seat of the Holy Roman Empire and a capital of artistic innovation. The Renaissance rebuilding of the castle was undertaken, under King Ferdinand I,

between 1526 and 1620, the year of the Battle of the White Mountain, which effectively ended the independence of the Czech state.

Under the Hapsburgs, the castle was again transformed. Between 1753 and 1775, under the direction of Maria Theresa, the castle was remodelled in a Neo-classical style. After this, the castle remained only a secondary residence of princes and was often deserted, finally becoming home to the last crowned Czech king, Emperor Ferdinand I, who lived there following his abdication until his death in 1875.

After the founding of the Republic in 1918, the castle was designated the Presidential Seat. In the 1920s, it was again remodelled and restored under the orders of President Masaryk, by Slovenian-born architect Josip Plečnik and his Czech associates 120. Within the castle walls are three gardens, also remodelled by Plečnik in the 1920s. Although during the war restoration work halted, it was continued under Communist rule. After 1989, President Havel arranged for the renewal and exhibition of Plečnik's contribution to the castle.

There are three main entrances to the palace: the north entrance by the Powder Bridge, the east from the Old Castle Steps, and the entrance leading from Hradčanské náměsti into the First Castle Courtyard. The first courtyard was built as part of Maria Theresa's remodelling of the castle in 1763–71, to the Neo-classical designs of Nicholas Pacassi in Vienna. With the team of architects Anselmo Lurago, Anton Kurz and Anton Haffenecker, Pacassi was responsible for the direction of the entire castle remodelling. Effectively the architects wrapped a unified Neo-classical skin around the varied assembly of earlier buildings, leaving certain key elements free. The Baroque **Mathias Gateway** (*illustration opposite*) of 1614 by G. Phillipi, which leads to the Second Courtyard, is framed in this way. The flagpoles and paving in front of the Gateway were part of Plečnik's renovation.

The shaping of Prague

Initially the **Second Castle Courtyard** was built outside of the castle fortifications in the sixteenth century, then connected to the interior in the years 1642–44. Again, Pacassi's modifications absorbed the courtyard more completely. Several buildings lead off this courtyard. The **Chapel of the Holy Cross** was the work of Lurago and Pacassi in 1756–63. The chapel's interiors were remodelled in 1852–56 in a Neo-Baroque style. It now houses the Treasury of St Vitus. On the north side of the courtyard is the Spanish Hall and Rudolf Gallery (1586–98). The Spanish Hall, the work of H. Fontana, was built in 1601–6 and was later modified by K. I. Dientzenhofer in 1748–50. Remodelling occurred again in 1865, in preparation for the abortive coronation of Franz Joseph I. Next to these state rooms is the Castle Art Gallery.

Second Castle Courtyard

The Third Castle Courtyard was the site of the original castle settlement, and the passage that leads to it once formed part of Soběslav's fortifications. The courtyard is dominated by the St Vitus Cathedral. To the right of the Cathedral's entrance is the **Old Provost's Lodge**, once the Bishop's Palace. The palace was constructed in the eleventh century, and its present exterior appearence was the result of the Baroque remodelling in 1662. The lodge's portal and corner statue of St Wenceslas were the work of Johann Bendl. The courtyard's obelisk was erected as a monument to the nation's war victims on the tenth anniversary of the Czechoslovak Republic in 1928 by Plečnik. Behind the obelisk is a Gothic bronze statue of St George from 1373, the work of George and Martin of Cluj. The Rococo façade of the south wing of the courtyard is the work of Pacassi, concealing earlier Renaissance and early Baroque buildings. In the south-east corner of the wing is the entrance to Plečnik's garden, Na Valech (on the ramparts).

Chapel of the Holy Cross

The origins of the **St Vitus Cathedral** date back to around 925, when Wenceslas I founded the Rotunda of St Vitus, which was replaced by a Romanesque basilica in the late eleventh century. The present Cathedral, however, was the centrepiece of Charles IV's 'Golden Age' – a magnificent construction that followed the pattern of southern French cathedrals. Charles IV, before his elevation to emperor, laid the foundation stone on 21 November 1334. In 1355, Charles acquired the remains of St Vitus and brought them to Prague from Pavia. The design of the new cathedral was initially the responsibility of the Frenchman, Matthias of Arras, who built the apse and eastern part of the choir before his death. After 1352, work continued under the guidance of Peter Parler. Parler's work in Prague, under the patronage of Charles IV, instigated a period of innovation and experimentation in late

Old Provost's Lodge

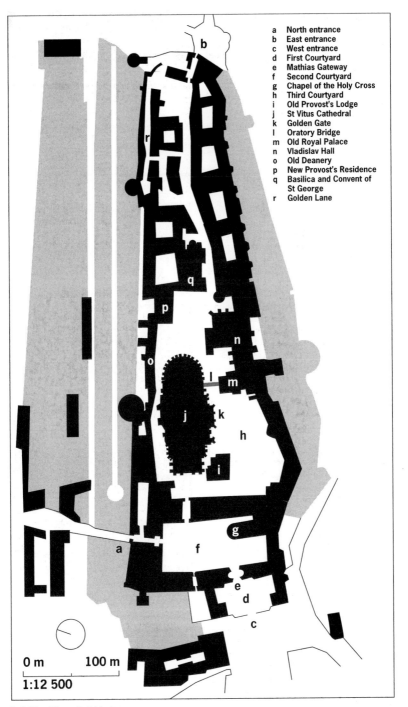

a   North entrance
b   East entrance
c   West entrance
d   First Courtyard
e   Mathias Gateway
f   Second Courtyard
g   Chapel of the Holy Cross
h   Third Courtyard
i   Old Provost's Lodge
j   St Vitus Cathedral
k   Golden Gate
l   Oratory Bridge
m   Old Royal Palace
n   Vladislav Hall
o   Old Deanery
p   New Provost's Residence
q   Basilica and Convent of
    St George
r   Golden Lane

0 m   100 m

1:12 500

Pražský hrad (Prague Castle) 1: plan

The shaping of Prague

St Vitus Cathedral

Golden Gate

Gothic design. Under Parler, the choir was completed and the south transept and part of the nave were built. Parler also began the main tower, adding the **Golden Gate**, or ceremonial entrance on the south side, opening into the courtyard. The gate is decorated with a mosaic depicting Bohemia's patron saints and Charles IV with his wife, created by Italian craftsmen in 1370.

Work on the tower was continued by Parler's sons, Wenceslas, John and Peter. During the Hussite wars, construction halted after the finished eastern part was closed by a temporary wall. Work began again after 1500, with the building of the Royal Oratory. In the 1560s, the main tower was completed by Bonifaz Wohlmut, who added the Renaissance parapet and onion dome. The dome was altered again by Pacassi in the 1770s. A century later the main structure of the cathedral was completed by Josef Kranner and Josef Mocker, in the spirit of nineteenth century revivalism and romanticism.

The interior of the cathedral is extremely impressive, in particular Parler's choir vaulting, which is a complex web as opposed to the more standard cross-rib vaults found in earlier buildings. The Chapel of St Wenceslas (1362–67), just inside the Golden Gate, was begun by Matthias but completed by Parler. The chapel covers the tomb of St Wenceslas, murdered on his way to mass in the original rotunda by his brother. The walls of the chapel were decorated in the 1370s with paintings of the Crucifixion, which are studded in areas with semi-precious stones. The chapel leads to the coronation chapel, in which are held the crown jewels.

Outside the cathedral at the south-east corner of the third courtyard is a bridge that leads from the cathedral to the castle buildings. The oratory was built for King Vladislav II Jagiello, and the bridge connected to his private rooms.

Leaving the third courtyard underneath the Oratory Bridge, the next complex of buildings is the **Old Royal Palace**, which was the residence of the Bohemian princes until the sixteenth century. The original palace was unified in a Gothic style in the late fifteenth century by Benedikt Ried, but much of his work was damaged in the great fire of 1541, which destroyed parts of the castle and the Lesser Town. Under the direction of Vladislav of Jagiello, Benedikt Ried (or Rejt) remodelled this and other parts of the castle in a late Gothic style.

Old Royal Palace

The entrance to the Palace is from the third court-yard, from which a number of small ante-rooms lead up to the impressive **Vladislav Hall**, built for Vladislav by Benedikt Ried between 1492–1502. The large hall occupies the whole of the second floor of the old palace; it is 62 metres long and 13 metres high. The hall, which has a delicate and sinuous rounded rib vault, leads at the east end to the Chapel of All Saints, originally built by Parler and remodelled after the fire in 1597. The Ludvik Wing, to the south of the hall, contains the Chancellery rooms. In 1618, the representatives of the Czech Estates threw the imperial governors from the windows of the Chancellery, an action which triggered the Thirty Years War. The Diet Hall, reached though a doorway in the north-east corner of the Vladislav Hall, is a complicated Gothic interior by Wohlmut, added after Ried's original interior was destroyed in the 1541 fire. Next to the Diet Hall is Ried's Late Gothic Riders Staircase of about 1500, built so that knights could enter Vladislav Hall for tournaments on horseback.

Underneath the Old Royal Palace is a remaining section of the medieval castle, including the Hall of the Romanesque Palace, which dates from the early twelfth century. At the entrance to this hall are elements of what is possibly the first ninth century castle. A staircase from the Hall of the Romanesque Palace leads to the ground floor of what was the palace of Charles IV. The first room is a vaulted hall,

Vladislav Hall

dating from the reign of Otakar II, which housed the Old Land Records; documents relating to the work of the Diet and to the ownership of property. Next to this, below the Vladislav Hall, are two halls from the former Gothic Palace of Charles IV. Beyond this are two further rooms, the Old Registry and Wenceslas IV's Hall of Columns, which dates from around 1400.

At the rear of St Vitus' Cathedral is St George's Square (Jiřské náměstí), linked to the Third Castle Courtyard by Vikářská street, which runs along the north side of the cathedral. In this street is the **Old Deanery**, a High Baroque 1705 building by Giovanni Santini-Aichl, which was built on the site of the original deanery, dating from 1483. Behind the deanery is Benedikt Ried's round artillery tower (the Mihulka Tower), which projects over the Deer Moat. Connecting Vikářská street to the square is a complex of nineteenth-century residences by Josef

Old Deanery

The shaping of Prague

New Provost's Residence

Mocker, including the Neo-Gothic **New Provost's Residence** of 1878. The main building dominating the square is the **Basilica and Convent of St George** (Bazilika sv. Jiří). The basilica was founded circa 915–20 by Vratislav I. When the convent was established by Boleslav II and his sister Mlada in about 973, the building was extended to a triple-naved basilica. After a fire in 1142, the twin towers were added to the basilica. The present early Baroque façade dates from 1657–80, the next major period of the reconstruction. (Next to this is the tiny Chapel of St John of Nepomuk, 1717–22.) The sixteenth century south portal of the basilica is the work of Benedikt Ried. The interior is probably the finest

Basilica and Convent of St George

example of Romanesque architecture and fresco decoration left in Bohemia, and has undergone extensive excavation and research. Masonry dating from the tenth century and the tombs of the early Přemyslid princes have been unearthed. The original arcades date from the tenth and eleventh centuries, the gallery windows from after 1142. The choir has remnants of Romanesque ceiling paintings. The little Chapel of St Ludmila contains a 1380s tomb made by the Parler Workshop, and frescoes from the sixteenth century. The Convent of St George was the first monastic house in Bohemia: the present construction was the result of rebuilding in 1657–60. In 1782, the convent was abolished and converted to barracks on the orders of Joseph II. In the 1970s, the building was adapted to serve as part of the National Gallery and now houses the collections of Bohemian art from Gothic to Baroque. The oldest surviving part of the convent is the Chapel of St Anne, built over the grave of the convent's founder, Mlada, and rebuilt in Baroque style in the 1670s.

On the corner of St George's Square that runs into Jiřská Street, is the site acquired by the Rožmberk family in 1545. The Italian architects, Giovanni Fontana and Ulrico Aostalli, were probably responsible for designing the Rožmberk Palace, a renaissance building with an arcaded courtyard, between 1545–73. The courtyard is all that remains of this palace. The present appearance of the palace dates from 1750s, when it was converted to an Institute for Impoverished Gentlewomen on the instructions of Maria Theresa, as part of Pacassi's large-scale homogenisation of the palace buildings.

Situated on Jiřská Street in the south-east corner of the castle is the Lobkowicz Palace. The palace is a group of buildings around a central courtyard, constructed in 1570. The exterior was reconstructed in an early Baroque manner by Carlo Lurago in 1651 for the Lobkowicz family. The exterior was remodelled again in 1791, although the pillared gateways

Golden Lane

and interiors remain from the sixteenth-century building. The palace is now part of the National Museum, and houses the collection that tells the history of the Czech lands.

Golden Lane (Zlatá Ulička) runs along the inside of the castle walls, between the Daliborka Tower (1496) and the New White Tower (1584). The lane is a pleasant ramshackle row of brightly coloured houses, now always busy with tourists who mill in and out of the numerous gift shops and commerical galleries. Once a street of goldsmiths, the street has had a rather bohemian reputation since the seventeenth century, as its cheap rents attracted artists and poets. Kafka lived in no. 22 during 1917, although the current appearance of the street is vastly different from the slum it would have been then.

From the sixteenth to the eighteenth centuries, the north side of the castle grounds, outside the walls, was a deer park; it is now crossed by the deep Deer Moat (Jelení příkop). The Royal Garden (Kralovská zahrada), which runs along the moat to the Belvedere (Kralovský Letohrádec) was founded in 1534 for Ferdinand I. At its entrance is the Lion Court, built for Rudolf II as a home for the emperor's collection of exotic animals, by Ulrico Aostalli in 1581–83. The Royal Garden also contains the Great Tennis Court, designed by Bonifaz Wohlmut between 1567–69. The building was damaged by fire in 1945 and subsequently restored by Paval Janák.

The shaping of Prague

2Bh **Vyšehrad Castle site** founded 10th century

V Pevnosti, Vyšehrad

M Vyšehrad; T 18, 24

The castle site at Vyšehrad was traditionally the first seat of the Přemyslid princes. On a high rocky outcrop above the Vltava to the south of the city, there have been fortifications there since the tenth century, if not longer. The royal use of the site was reinstated by Charles IV, who planned his coronation ceremony in 1347 to start at Vyšehrad and then travel to the Prague Castle. Excavations this century have shown the plan of the royal palace there, which was abandoned and in ruins by the end of the sixteenth century. Plans and engravings of the castle show that it was once as grand as Prague Castle itself. Much of the medieval site had been destroyed in the Hussite Wars, and by later redevelopment. The medieval fortifications were replaced by a new system of walls and battlements in the seventeenth century, and other Baroque modifications were made in the eighteenth. Most of the early buildings have been rebuilt or remodelled except for the **Rotunda of St Martin**, the oldest surviving building at Vyšehrad, probably dating from the second half of the eleventh century. Built during the first phase of the area's importance, in the reign of Vratislav II, it served as the church for the outer bailey. The tiny chapel inside was altered between 1878–80 by A. Baum, when the Neo-Romanesque entrance was added, decorated with scenes taken from an eleventh century illuminated manuscript.

The dominant building on the Vyšehrad site, the **Church of Sts Peter and Paul**, dates back to the eleventh century. The Přemyslid rulers were buried in the crypt of the original basilica, which was destroyed and replaced by a Gothic church at the end of the fourteenth century. The eighteenth-century remodelling has been obscured by the Neo-Gothic reconstruction of the 1870s.

The eleventh-century **Basilica of St Lawrence**, on Soběslavova Street was rebuilt several times after it was almost destroyed in the fifteenth century. Since then, excavation has uncovered not only some of the original eleventh-century flooring (now in the Lapidarum), but also evidence of an even earlier sacred site. The basilica's Baroque appearance dates from 1753–73. Other smaller buildings were added during the eighteenth-century remodelling, including the Baroque Chapel of Our Lady (Kaple Panny Marie v hradbách), built in the 1760s.

Vyšehrad enjoyed a revival of interest in the nineteenth century, as its romantic character and mythic associations appealed to the national revival movement. Several Gothic Revival buildings were added during the 1870s. It now has a peaceful and relaxed atmosphere, attracting tourists who come to wander around the churches and gardens and take in the wonderful views of the Vltava. There are several cafés and galleries, usually busy in the summer months. To get there, walk up the hill through the Brickworks Gate (Cihlová brána) along V Pevnosti Street. The gate was built as part of the military defences in 1841.

3Ak Rotunda of the Holy Rood
early 12th century
Karoliny světle, Staré Město

M Národní Třída

This Romanesque rotunda was constructed at a point along the medieval riverside route from Vyšehrad to the main river crossing, near the Charles Bridge. The rotunda – usually about six metres in diameter, with a conical roof and lantern window – is the earliest surviving form of religious building. There are two other examples of Romanesque rotundas in the city: the Rotunda of St Martin at Vyšehrad, and the Rotunda of St Longinus, Na Rybníčku Street, Nové Město. The Rotunda of the Holy Rood has some remaining fragments of four-teenth-century wall painting, which were preserved as part of the redecoration of the building in the 1870s, when it was restored by I. V. Ullmann.

4Ag House of the Lords of Kunštát and Poděbrady
c. 1150–1250
Řetězová 3/946, Staré Město

M Národní Třída

Over the last century, reconstruction and excava-tion has revealed a number of Romanesque dwell-ings in the heart of the city. Most would have been three storeys high, with a workshop lower ground floor reached by an external staircase. The lower floors were often incorporated into Gothic and Baroque town houses, but the original buildings are rarely visible from the exterior. One of the few examples of Romanesque domestic architecture accessible to the public is this house on Řetězová. This building contains the original two-storey dwell-ing, now encased by a Neo-classical reconstruction. The basement and ground floors are accessible, and are now a café and art gallery, with an exhibition of the history of the house. The basement has three interconnected rooms with vaulted ceilings. The house was at one time the home of Jiří of Poděbrady, inherited from his uncle, Lord Bocek of Kunštát.

5Ac Convent of St Agnes c. 1233–80
Anežská Street 12/811–4, Staré Město

M Staroměstká

The convent is the oldest Gothic complex of build-ings in Prague, founded in 1233 by Agnes (or Anežská) of Bohemia, sister of Wenceslas I. It be-came the home of the Franciscan Order of the Poor Clares, with Agnes as abbess. The east wing of the convent has a brick northern gable, and inside there is a chapter hall, with an early Gothic joist ceiling, in front of a vaulted refectory. The convent was ex-tended in the fourteenth century, when an extra storey was added on the wings of the cloister. The

The shaping of Prague

convent was deserted during the Hussite revolution of 1420, until it was occupied by the Dominicans a century later, and the Poor Clares returned in 1627. Abandoned again at the end of the eighteenth century, it was used as a poorhouse before restoration attempts began in 1892. Since 1980, the convent has been the home of the national collection of nineteenth-century fine and applied arts.

The complex of buildings includes the church of St Francis (1234), which was extended in the 1350s.

By the sixteenth century the church was almost in ruins, with only the early Gothic presbytery remaining. After archaeological investigations in the 1940s and 1950s, the church was fully restored, with a new roof, in 1985–86. The Church of the Holy Saviour, with a chapel dedicated to Mary Magdalen (1270–80), and the fourteenth-century Chapel of St Barbara were also restored in the 1980s. Archaeological research during restoration uncovered many royal remains, including the tomb of King Wenceslas I.

6Ag **Old–New Synagogue** c. 1280
Červená, Josefov

M Staroměstská

This is one of the best-preserved synagogues in Europe and the oldest of those remaining in central Prague. The Old–New synagogue was once the centre of Jewish life in the ghetto, and is still used for worship today. Originally, the site of the synagogue was significantly higher than the surrounding buildings, although this difference is hardly noticeable now, as the streets were levelled during the rebuilding of Josefov in the nineteenth century. The core of the building is the oldest part; a lower hall with two pillars supporting the vault which is in six sections, each with five ribs. This hall is reached by the entrance to the side of the building, through the carved doorway decorated with a vine motif, dating from the thirteenth century. The brick gables at the end of the building facing away from Pařížská were added in the fourteenth century. The side corridor with small windows looking into the main hall was added in the seventeenth century, apparently so that women could observe some services. In the 1880s, the synagogue underwent some reconstruction, carried out by the architect Josef Mocker. Mocker stripped the interior of its decoration, in a mistaken attempt to 'return' the building to what was considered its original appearance. Further

work in the 1960s uncovered some of the fresco work in the main hall.

There are six synagogues remaining within the site of the Old Ghetto. The other five are: the **High Synagogue**, also on Červená 5/101; the **Maisel Synagogue**, Maislova 10/63; the **Pinkas Synagogue**, Široká 3/23; the Baroque **Klausen Synagogue**, U starého hřbitova 1; and the **Spanish Synagogue** 55.

7Ag **Old Town Hall** 1338 onwards
Staroměstské náměstí 3/1, Staré Město

M Staroměstská

The Old Town Hall (Staroměstská Radnice) with its famous clock tower which attracts crowds on the hour every day, is an amalgamation of several residences that stood on the site prior to 1338, when King John of Luxembourg granted administrative autonomy to the old town of Prague. The first dwelling to be purchased to house the new (later old) town hall in that year was the Volflin House, and

the clock tower was added. Other plots surrounding the town hall were subsequently purchased and adapted, including the Kříž house (1387), the Mikš House (1548) and the early Gothic dwelling U Kohouta, incorporated in the 1830s. These make up the south façade of the town hall. Although the appearance of a cluster of buildings rather than a unified whole is clear, not all the original features of the former buildings remain. The Gothic doorway of the Wolflin House, next to the clock tower, is an example. Decorated Gothic doorways and windows and some work by the sculptor Matéj Rejsek were added as the complex grew. The tower itself is nearly 60 metres tall, with a chapel on the first floor,

which has an oriel window overlooking the square, on the east façade of the tower. The clock dates from the 1780s (with additions in the 1860s), although there had been a clock in that position since the fifteenth century. In the 1910s and 1930s, minor alterations and restoration works were undertaken by leading architects, including Jan Kotěra and later Pavel Janák. The north wing, added at the beginning of the nineteenth century, was completely destroyed by bombing in 1945. This site was subsequently the focus of several architectural competitions (the last in 1984), but none were carried out.

8Ag Church of Our Lady before the Týn
1339 onwards
Staroměstské náměstí, Staré Město

M Staroměstská

One of Prague's best known architectural landmarks, the Gothic spires of Týn Church provide a stark contrast to the Baroque façades of the Old Town Square. There are mentions of a Romanesque church belonging to a hostel for foreign merchants on this site, dating from 1135. The hostel of the Týn was located to the east of the existing church, within a complex known as the Ungelt. This complex contained the customs house and a number of burgher's houses, and surrounds a courtyard with two gateways. On the site of the original building is a Renaissance palace dating from 1560, built for the duty collector, Jakob Granovský.

The construction of the existing church was begun in 1339 by architects Peter Schmelzer and Otto Scheuffler, and replaced an Early Gothic version dating from the thirteenth century. By the 1380s the side naves and the masonry of the main nave were complete. The towers, with their projecting turrets, were completed and the west gable added following the Hussite Wars. Building work resumed after 1457, continuing until the early sixteenth century. The sculptural and decorative work, including the doorway on the north side, was very likely the work of Peter Parler's court workshop between 1390 and 1410. The interior is still rich in Gothic decoration, some of it by Matéj Rejsek, who taught at the adjacent Týn School 20. The church was a centre of reformist activity during the Hussite

Wars. George of Poděbrady had a statue of himself with a gold chalice placed on the façade as a symbol of the Utraquist cause, but this was replaced with a figure of the Virgin in 1626, with the gold melted down and reused. Some subsequent additions were made, including the Baroque vault of the central nave, which was added after fire damaged the interior in 1679. Some nineteenth-century alteration is visible, including the Neo-Gothic St Luke's altar. The church is reached through an arcade leading from the Týn School, an early Gothic building modified in the sixteenth century.

The shaping of Prague

9Ao **'Na Slovanech' Abbey** founded 1347
Vyšehradská 49/320, Nové Město

M Karlovo náměstí

The monastery was founded by Charles IV for the Slav Benedictines, intended to demonstrate the political commitment of the throne to this tradition of regional Czech worship. The new monastery, which also became known by the local name of Emmaus, was given this prominent site in the New Czech town, and housed many important medieval documents in Old Slavonic and Czech languages. Work on the monastery and church was completed by 1372. The hall type church was 50 metres long, with a high roof topped with a small turret rather than towers. To the south side of the church is the medieval cloister which has 22 groin-vaulted bays. In the seventeenth century the monastery buildings were rebuilt in a Baroque manner, and two domed towers added to the western façade of the church. Within the complex there is also the small Baroque chapel of Sts Cosmas and Damian. Heavily damaged during the 1945 bombings, the western façade of the church was reconstructed with two new spires 171. The medieval cloister had been decorated with fresco cycles dating from 1360–70 by artists from Charles IV's court, but these were also badly damaged in 1945, and despite restoration only fragments of the original wall paintings remain.

10Ag **Carolinum University** founded 1348
Železná no. 9/541, Staré Město

M Staroměstská

The Carolinum is the central building of the Charles University, the first university in Central Europe, established by Charles IV on 7 April 1348. Although at first the new university did not have a building of its own, lectures took place in various churches and monasteries in the city. In 1366, Charles College was founded in the Old Town. The buildings originally on this site were donated to the college in 1383 by Wenceslas IV, and the site was expanded to form the centralised university by the early fifteenth century. In 1718, architect F. M. Kaňka gave the buildings a unified Baroque appearance, leaving only one fragment of the original building – the beautiful Gothic oriel window in the southern façade, overlooking Ovocný trh (the old Fruit Market). Between 1881–82, Josef Mocker modified the Carolinum again, this time employing a Neo-Gothic style. From 1946–65, the building was returned to an approximation of Kaňka's plan by Jaroslav Fragner, reconstructing the interiors and relocating the entrance to Ovocný trh. For this task, Fragner

was awarded the status of 'National Artist'. The first stage of redevelopment began with the restoration of the Assembly Hall, and the addition of a new foyer and other necessary facilities. The complex was extended to include university buildings on Celetná. After the restoration of the courtyard, Fragner added a new building to house the University Rectorate, which created a strikingly modern entrance to the whole complex. The new building is set back to provide a three sided 'courtyard', opening out into the street to connect rather than separate the university complex from the city. The building sits in deference to its surroundings and is an example of how modern architecture can be used with success in a historic location.

11Af Charles Bridge from 1357

Peter Parler

M Staroměstská

Charles Bridge, originally Prague Bridge and re-named in 1870, was built to the requirements of Charles IV and supervised by Peter Parler in the mid-to-late fourteenth century. It occupies the site of the main river crossing between the Old and New Towns, and had been the site of a bridge from as early as the eleventh century. The first stone bridge to be built there, Judith Bridge (1158–60), was destroyed by flood in 1342, although indications of it remain, including one tower on the Malá Štrana side (now part of the Monastery of the Knights of the Cross).

On the Staré Město side is the Old Town Bridge Tower (leading to Křižovnické náměstí), the large gateway built by Parler, and damaged in the war against the Swedes in 1648. The tower bears the coats of arms of the members of the Czech king-dom, including those of the Czech king and Roman emperor. There is also a statue of St Vitus, the bridge's patron saint, flanked on the right by a throned statue of Charles IV and on the left by Wenceslas IV. The tower's gateway is vaulted, with the Czech crown at its centre. The tower was restored by Josef Mocker in the 1870s, when it was given its present roof. It is open to the public in the summer.

The sixteen-arch bridge, built of sandstone, is deco-rated with thirty sculptures, mainly dating from the Baroque period, with certain nineteenth-century additions. Some of these are copies, with the originals now held in the National Museum's Lapidarium.

On the Malá Strana side are the two Lesser Town Bridge towers. The lower south tower was rebuilt in a Renaissance style in 1591, although based around the earlier Romanesque tower, originally built in the twelfth century. The higher north tower was built to complement Parler's Gothic tower on the opposite side after 1464 and under the direction of King George of Poděbrady.

Details of the the bridge's sculptures, beginning from the Old Town Bridge tower, are shown at right.

First Pier: *St Ivo*, 1711, M. Braun (left). *The Virgin and St Bernard*, 1709, M. Jäckel (right).
Second Pier: *Sts Barbara, Margaret and Elizabeth*, 1707, F. Brokoff (left). *The Virgin, Sts Dominic and Aquinas*, 1708 , M. Jäckel (right).
Third Pier: *Pietá group*, 1859, E. Max (left). *Gilt and Stone Crucifix group*, 1629, H. Hillger, and 1861, E. Max (right).
Fourth Pier: *St Joseph*, 1854, J. Max (left). *St Ann with Jesus*, 1707, M. Jäckel (right).
Fifth Pier: *St Francis Xavier*, 1711, F. Brokoff (left). *Sts Cyril and Methodius*, 1938, K. Dvořák (right).
Sixth Pier: *St Christopher*, 1857, E. Max (left). *St John the Baptist*, 1857, J. Max (right).
Seventh Pier: *St Francis Borgia*, 1710, F. Brokoff (left). *Sts Wenceslas, Norbert and Sigismund*, 1853, J. Max (right).
Eighth Pier: *Sts Ludmilla and Wenceslas*, c. 1720, workshop of B. Braun (left). *St John Nepomuk*, 1673, M. Rauchmüller and J. Brokoff (right).
Ninth Pier: *St Francis of Assisi*, 1855, E. Max (left). *St Anthony of Padua*, 1707, J. Mayer (right).
Tenth Pier: *Sts Vincent Ferrer and Procopius*, 1712, F. Brokoff (left). *St Jude Thaddaeus*, 1708, J. Mayer (right).
Eleventh Pier: *St Nicholas of Tolentino*, 1708, J. F. Kohl (left). *St Augustine*, 1708, J. F. Kohl (right).
Twelfth Pier: *St Luitgard*, 1710, M. Braun (left). *St Catejan*, 1709, F. Brokoff (right).
Thirteenth Pier: *St Adalbert*, 1709, possibly F. Brokoff (left). *St Philip Benitius*, 1714, M. Mandl (right).
Fourteenth Pier: *Sts John of Matha, Felix of Valois, Ivan and a Turkish Guard*, 1714, F. Brokoff (left). *St Vitus*, 1714, F. Brokoff (right).

The shaping of Prague

12Ai Hunger Wall 1360–62
Petřinské Sady, Malá Strana

T 12, 27

Snaking up Petřín Hill from Újezd Street to Strahov is the Hunger Wall (Hladová zeď), a Gothic fortification wall so-called because it was built at the request of Charles IV by the city's poor, providing them with some sort of living. The wall is punctuated with ramps and battlements for the defence of the Lesser Town. If the climb is too much, it is best viewed by taking the funicular railway up the hill.

13Ak New Town Hall 1367 onwards
Karlovo náměstí 23/1, Nové Město

M Karlovo náměstí

The New Town Hall (Novoměstská Radnice), probably begun in 1367, if not earlier, looked after administration for the town that Charles IV founded in 1348. The significance of the site (a busy cattle market) was reinforced when Charles decreed that the coronation procession would cross it on its way from Vyšehrad to the castle. The earliest surviving building, however, dates from the years 1411–18 when it was rebuilt under the supervision of Master Kříž. On the ground floor, in the gabled wing facing Charles Square, is a large Gothic entrance hall that was built at this time. The building's tower was added in 1425, and a number of further alterations took place in the sixteenth century, including the addition of a gabled façade. After the building ceased to function as a town hall in 1784 it became a criminal court and prison. Other subsequent minor alterations took place, including the removal of the Renaissance gables, which were replaced during restoration in 1905 by Antonín Wiehl and Kamil Hilbert. Considerable restoration and archaeological work was also done in the 1970s.

14Af Church of Our Lady Below the Chain 1370s
Lázenská, Malá Strana

M Malostranská

The peculiar name of this church (Kostel Panny Marie pod řetězem) comes from the heavy chain originally used to open the monastery gate. The Monastery of the Order of the Knights of St John (or Knights of Malta as they became known) was founded here after land was granted to the knights by Vladislav II in 1169. The knight's fortified monastery was strategically placed to protect the approach to the Judith Bridge. Initially a much larger Romanesque church (c. 1169–82) stood on the site (fragments of the Romanesque arcade can be seen embedded in the walls of the courtyard), to which a Gothic presbytery was added in the thirteenth century. The rest of the Romanesque building was demolished to make way for a new Gothic building – only part of this plan was ever executed. The vestibule was built circa 1375, and the massive square towers added in about 1389. The nave was never built; instead, a courtyard was created inside the complex between the towers and the actual church at the rear. Between 1640 and 1660, Carlo Lurago made some Baroque alterations to the church.

15Ag Church of Our Lady of the Snows and Monastery c. 1379
Jungmannovo náměstí, Nové Město

M Müstek

Founded by Charles IV for the Carmelites in 1347, the church (Kostel Panny Marie Sněžné) on the corner of Jungmann Square was originally intended to be the largest church of its time in the city. It was planned as a triple naved church, 110 metres long, but only the central nave, nearly 40 metres high, was completed. Construction of the church did not begin until 1379, by which time the monastery was completed on the southern side of the church site. The presbytery was finished by 1397, but building work was halted before the church reached its intended size. The steeple at the northern end of the presbytery was added in the fifteenth century. In the sixteenth century, the monastery was partially abandoned, and reconstruction began under the Franciscans in the seventeenth century. The delicate net vaulting of the nave was added in 1606. In 1788, the courtyard of the church was completed in a Neo-classical style. The monastery gardens next door were reconstructed in the 1950s, creating an access between Jungmann Square and the streets adjoining Wenceslas Square. The interior of the church is currently undergoing restoration. The courtyard buildings have recently been renovated, and now serve as the Austrian Cultural Institute.

The shaping of Prague

16Ag **Bethlehem Chapel** 1391–94/1948–54
Betlémské náměstí, Staré Město
Jaroslav Fragner

M Národni Třída

The present building is a reconstruction, from plans and prints, of the original fourteenth-century chapel, carried out by Jaroslav Fragner at the request of the Czech government in 1950–54, as a monument to the Hussite Movement and the Czech Reformation. The original two-gabled building was founded by Hanuš of Mühlheim as a centre for worship in the Czech language. Subsequently the ideological centre of the reformation, Jan Hus preached here between 1402–13. Thomas Müntzer, the protestant theologian and leader of the German Peasant's Revolt, wrote his 'Prague Manifesto' while preaching here in 1521. A Jesuit chapel in the seventeenth and eighteenth centuries, the Bethlehem Chapel was demolished after the suppression of the Jesuits in 1773. The reconstruction of the chapel is an interesting example of the exploitation of Czech national history by the Communist government of the 1950s, in choosing to commemorate Müntzer's revolutionary activities. The chapel now houses a museum dedicated to Hus's work. In the courtyard next to the chapel is a new architecture gallery, named after Fragner. The gallery exhibits recent projects and competitions from the Czech Republic and abroad. There is a restaurant downstairs.

17Ah **Powder Tower (Prašná Brána)** 1475
Náměstí Republiky, Nové Město

M Náměstí Republiky

The Powder Tower is the only remaining one of the medieval gates into the Old Town. The foundation stone was laid by Vladislav II in 1475. The architect was Matéj Rejsek, who took over the building of the tower in 1478, although it was never fully completed. The design of the Tower was based on Peter Parler's Charles Bridge Tower 11. After serving as a gunpowder store during the eighteenth century, it was badly damaged during the Prussian siege. Its recent appearance is largely the work of that prolific Neo-Gothic revivalist, Josef Mocker, who reconstructed the tower in 1875–86.

18Ae Schwarzenberg Palace 1545–63

Hradčanské náměstí 2/185, Hradčany

Augustin Vlach

M Hradčanska

The major fire in 1541 that destroyed much of the medieval building surrounding the castle and the Lesser Town left land ready for development. This site on the south side of Hradčany Square was acquired by Jan of Lobkowicz soon after. He commissioned Augustin Vlach to build this impressive Renaissance palace. The façade was decorated in 1567 with sgraffito rustication, a style borrowed from Northern Italy but also characteristic of Bohemian Renaissance architecture, as is the gabled parapet. The façade decoration has been reconstructed on two occasions, once in 1871–93 by Josef Schulz, and again in the 1950s.

The interiors of the palace are impressive, with decorated panel ceilings and several series of paintings with mythological scenes. After passing through several hands, the palace became the property of the Schwarzenbergs in the eighteenth century. It now houses the Museum of Military History.

19Ab Belvedere (Královský Letohrádek) 1537–63

U Prašného mostu, Hradčany

Paolo della Stella and Bonifaz Wohlmut

M Hradčanska

The pleasure gardens to the east of the castle site were planned in the 1530s on a terrace beyond the Stag Moat. The Belvedere, or summer palace, was built by Ferdinand I for his wife, Anna, employing the Genoese architect, Paolo della Stella, who designed the villa while still in Italy. Stella came to Prague in 1538, employing a team of Italian stonemasons to realise his design. When he died in 1552, the ground floor of the villa, with its arcaded loggia, was complete. The upper floors, with a balustraded terrace, were completed to Stella's plans by his successor Wohlmut, who also added the elegant curving roof. Stella's designs are reminiscent of Serlio and Palladio, and the Belvedere is the earliest example of an Italian villa in Bohemia. The relief decoration around the colonnade was Stella's, and among the historical and mythological imagery, Ferdinand is depicted with his wife, Anna.

Wohlmut, a German architect from Baden, came to Prague in 1554 as the new royal architect. His completion of the villa marked a change to a more solid and monumental Mannerist style. The villa has had several subsequent alterations. The interior was remodelled in 1841–55 by Nobile and Grueber, who added the monumental staircase at the north end. In the 1950s, the villa was restored by Pavel Janák, who had previously reconstructed the garden in the 1930s.

The Renaissance garden, or *giardinetto*, has at its centre the **Singing Fountain**, by Francesco Terzio, cast by Tomáš Jaroš in 1564.

The shaping of Prague

20Ag **Týn School and the House of the White Unicorn** c. 1562

Staroměstské náměstí 14 & 16/604 & 605, Staré Město

M Staroměstská

This Renaissance façade dates from the mid sixteenth century, when the original Gothic building was remodelled. From the fourteenth century until the mid nineteenth century, the building was occupied by the highly regarded parish school, where the architect Matéj Rejsek taught in the fifteenth century. Inside, the Gothic rib-vaults are still visible. The arcade, which connects the school to the House of the White Unicorn next door, dates from the fourteenth century. What is most interesting about the building is its gabled façade, raised to hide the original medieval roof. Although this style of stepped gabling shows the influence of Venetian Renaissance forms, it also echoes the Gothic character of the Týn church **8** behind it. Presumably, these were, at one point, almost identical. The House of the White Unicorn was remodelled in the eighteenth century and an extra storey was added in the nineteenth century in place of its gabled parapet.

21Be **Hvězda (Star) Palace** 1555–56
Liboc
Hans Tirol and Bonifaz Wohlmut

T 8

On the hillside close to the site of the famous Battle of the White Mountain (Bílá Hora) is this summer hunting lodge, built for Archduke Ferdinand of the Tyrol, son of Ferdinand I. The work was carried out under the direction of Hans Tirol by Italians, Juan Maria del Pambio and Giovanni Lucchese, and was completed by Bonifaz Wohlmut. Ferdinand's original design is preserved in National Library of Vienna. The palace is in the form of a six-pointed star, with a polygonal central room. Each point contains a rhomboid shaped room, accessible by narrow corridors that radiate out from the central space. The interior stucco decoration was the work of Italian masters, Giovanni Campione and Andrea Avostolis del Pambio. The walled grounds in their current state were laid out in the English style of

landscaping in 1787. The palace is now a museum dedicated to the work of the writer Alois Jiráska (1851–1930) and the painter Mikoláš Aleš (1852–1913), both of whom were important to the growth of a Czech national movement at the end of the nineteenth century. The palace has been extensively and sensitively restored, apart from the addition of a somewhat incongruous lecture theatre.

22Ae Hradčanská Radnice (Hradčany Town Hall)
1601–4

Loretánská 1/173, Hradčany

M Hradčanska

After Hradčany was given the status of Royal Town
in 1598, the new town hall was built on this site. The
sgraffito decoration on the façade would have been
typical of much building of the period, but on many
it was covered over with stucco when buildings were
given a Baroque facelift a century or so later. The
building also carries remnants of its former status
as town hall (which ceased in 1784): the fragments
of the imperial coat of arms, the Hradčany emblem
and the painting of Justice.

Valdštejn Palace and Gardens, 23

An era of sumptuous display 1620–1800

23Af Valdštejn Palace and Gardens 1621–30
Valdštejnské náměstí 4/17, Malá Strana
Andrea Spezza

M Malostranská

Over 20 houses were cleared for the site of the earliest grand Baroque palace in Prague. The Commander of the imperial Catholic Army, Albrecht von Wallenstein (or Valdštejn), purchased the land, which contained an existing Renaissance mansion, with the intention of building a palace finer than even the Royal Palace. A team of Italian architects, under the control of Andrea Spezza, were commissioned to create a grand palace with five courtyards and formal gardens (which can be reached through the entrance in Letenská). The late Renaissance façade that faces onto Valdštejnské náměstí incorporates the grand gates, probably inspired by the castle's own Mathias Gate. The exterior of the

palace is rather restrained in comparison with the grand interior (generally closed to the public). The focal point of the interior plan is the two-storey Hall of the Knights, with a 1630 ceiling fresco by Baccio di Bianco. The garden contains a grand, three-arcade sala terrena at the westerly end, with ceiling painting again by Bianco. The arcade was designed by Giovanni Pierroni in 1630.

The palace remained in the Wallenstein family until 1945, when it became the property of the state. It now houses various government offices and the Komensky Pedagogical Museum. The gardens are open to the public and used in the summer months for musical events. The intention was to create gardens reminiscent of ancient Rome, in particular the aviary grotto, an immense wall fashioned to look like stalactites. At the opposite end of the gardens to the palace is the Riding School, which is now a gallery for twentieth-century art exhibitions.

24Af Michna Palace 1631–50
Újezd 40/450, Malá Strana
Francesco Caratti

M Malostranská; T 12, 22

This extravagant palace was planned by Pavel Michna, an imperial Army officer, who bought the Renaissance summer palace on this site in 1623 and began its conversion following the example of his superior, Albrecht von Wallenstein. The original palace was not demolished, but extended on all sides, its arcades filled in to create a sequence of rooms. Caratti used a team of Italian craftsmen to decorate the palace to a very high standard. The garden wing of the palace was never completed, although later the gardens were extended to reach as far as Kampa Island. As happened to many other palaces, the Michna Palace suffered considerable neglect when it became the property of the military in the late eighteenth century. Since the 1920s, it

has been the home of the Czech sports and culture organisation, Sokol, and houses a hostel, sports facilities and an exhibition area.

An era of sumptuous display

25Af Schönborn Palace 1643–1718

Tržiště 15/365, Malá Strana

Carlo Lurago

M Malostranská

The Schönborn Palace was another early Baroque palace, although its appearance dates from when it was rebuilt around 1715. Lurago was commissioned by the Colloredo family in the mid seventeenth century, although all that remains of his work is the impressive entrance gate. Between 1715–18 the family had the palace remodelled by Bartolomeo Scotti, probably to plans by either Giovanni Santini-Aichl or Giovanni Alliprandi. The palace is now the US Embassy, and both palace and its famous gardens are closed to the public. The gardens were designed by landscape gardener M. Lebesche, who was responsible for several grand garden projects in the early eighteenth century. It is possible to view the gardens from a distance from the slopes of Petřín Hill.

26Ae Černín Palace 1668–1720

Loretánské náměstí 5/101, Hradčany

Francesco Caratti

M Hradčanská; T 22

The palace was built for Jan Humbrecht Černín von Chudenitz, the imperial ambassador to Venice. Although the chief architect of the palace was Francesco Caratti, it has been suggested that preliminary sketches were made by Bernini, whom Černín met during his time in Italy. Caratti's monumental design is in the style of an Italianate palazzo and has a basement storey with diamond rustication. It is highly likely that Černín intended his new palace to rival those of the emperor in Vienna. The massive façade (135 metres long) has thirty Corinthian half columns running the length of the building, with twenty-nine window bays. After Caratti, a succession of architects worked on the palace, most importantly František Kaňka, who from 1718 added the monumental staircase and the Orangery, and also laid out the gardens. Anselmo Lurago completed the façade with a balcony across the central three entrance bays in 1744–49, but only after the palace had been badly plundered by the French in 1742. The palace was severely damaged again during the Prussian bombardment of 1757. In the nineteenth century, when the building served as a barracks, it fell into disrepair. It was restored by Pavel Janák in 1928–34, who added the modern brick western wing. Following this, Janák also reconstructed the gardens in 1934–35. During World War II the palace served as headquarters to the Nazis; since then it has housed the Foreign Ministry.

27Ae Strahov Monastery 1682–98

Strahovské Nádvoří, Hradčany

Jean-Baptiste Mathey

M Hradčanská; T 22

The complex of buildings known as the Strahov Monastery dates back to the twelfth century, although the abbey and some of the surrounding buildings were extensively remodelled by the Baroque architect, Mathey, in the late seventeenth century. The original Romanesque monastery had been destroyed by fire in 1258 and was swiftly rebuilt. Between 1614 and 1629, Abbott Questenberg had the Abbey remodelled in a Renaissance style. Two chapels date from the earlier period: the small Kostel sv. Rocha (Church of St Roch), which dates from 1603–12, and the main Kostel Nanebevzetí Panny Marie (Assumption of the Virgin), which dates from 1148, was altered by Mathey. Mathey's work at Strahov had been damaged during the siege of Prague in 1741, but it still defines the character of the present complex. The famous Neo-classical library was converted from a former granary by Palliardi in 1783. Inside the library is Palliardi's two storey Philosophical Hall, a magnificent Baroque interior (1783–90), which is now the National Museum of Literature. The ceiling fresco in the Philosophical Hall is by the Viennese painter, Franz Anton Maulpertsch. The hall was built to incorporate the library of Louka, which had been acquired, complete with shelving, for Prague. Beyond Palliardi's hall is the Theological Hall, built by Giovanni Domenico Orsi in the 1670s, shortly before Mathey's work began. The two halls are linked by a *trompe l'oeil* corridor. From the monastery grounds, leading onto Petřín Hill, there are impressive views over the city.

28Ae Tuscany Palace 1689–91

Hradčanské náměstí 5/182, Hradčany

Jean-Baptiste Mathey

M Hradčanská

This early Baroque palace (originally known as the Thun-Hohenstein Palace) most probably was designed by Jean-Baptiste Mathey for Michal Osvald, Count Thun-Hohenstein, and bought by Maria-Anna, Grand Duchess of Tuscany, in 1718. The façade is decorated with two columned portals and shallow pilasters by every window. Above the two doorways are pavilion roofs to complete the symmetry of the façade. On the attic storey there are figures representing the liberal arts, by Johann Brokoff, and two large sculpted coats of arms; those

of Tuscany and the duke of Tuscany's family arms. The figure of St Michael in a stucco frame on the corner of the building is by the Italian sculptor, Ottavio Mosto, and dates from 1694. Inside the building there are fine frescoed ceilings, from around 1700. The whole palace was restored in the 1940s.

An era of sumptuous display

29Ag St František Church 1679–89
Křižovnické náměstí, Staré Město
Jean-Baptiste Mathey

M Staroměstská

This small Baroque church close to the Charles Bridge was built on the site of an early triple-naved Gothic church, once the property of the Knights of the Cross. Part of the original church was incorporated into the crypt of the new church. The rather remarkable dome of Mathey's church is constructed of four arms which extend from an elliptical central space below. The façade is decorated with statuary representing the Czech patron saints, probably the work of Andreas Quittainer in the 1720s. The attic storey angels (now replaced by copies) are the work of M. Jäckel. On the corner with Křižovnická is a monument, once part of the Guild of Winegrowers's building, which now has a statue of St Wenceslas dating from 1676, by Johann George Bendl. Surrounding the base of the monument is part of the original paving from the Judith Bridge, the predecessor of the Charles Bridge.

30Ag Clementium 1654–58
Křižonovnické náměstí, Staré Město
Carlo Lurago

M Staroměstská

This large complex of buildings was built on the site of a monastery which dated from 1232, when the Dominicans erected a friary next to the Romanesque church of St Clement. In its present state, it is one of the finest demonstrations of the range and development of Bohemian Baroque. Following the Battle of the White Mountain in 1620, the site became the notional centre of the Counter-Reformation, housing the Jesuit college and monastical headquarters. Between 1593 and 1601, the triple-naved Church of St Saviour was built in the Renaissance style; it is the oldest Jesuit church in Prague. Then, in 1653–60, the architect, Carlo Lurago, added the range of college buildings on Křižonovnicka, after designs by Francesco Caratti. The north range of buildings (facing Platernská) was built by Domenico Orsi in 1660–64. The eastern section was begun in 1721 by František Kaňka, possibly with the cooperation of K. I. Dientzenhofer. This wing contains the Jesuit Library, which has barley-sugar columns, and a fresco ceiling (1727) by Johann Heibl. Kaňka also added the observatory tower (1721), built to house the astronomical research activities of J. Steepling, and the Chapel of Mirrors (1724) to the east wing. The chapel has stucco decoration into which mirrors have been inserted. It is accessible for concerts and other events.

The original Romanesque Church of St Clement (on Karlova) was replaced in 1711–15 by the Baroque building of K. I. Dientzenhofer. The interior contains a ceiling fresco of St Clement by Johann Heibl, and wooden sculptural decoration (seen in the side altars, font and choir) from the studio of Mathias Braun. The St Linhart altar painting is by P. J. Brandl. To the side of St Clement is the Italian Chapel, dating from 1590–1600. The portico and iron work of the chapel's doorway is also by Kaňka, and dates from 1715.

After the suppression of the Jesuits in 1773, the Clementium passed eventually to the Prague University in 1777. It now houses the various departments of the State Library. The Church of St Clement was restored in 1980, and is now used by the Greek-Catholic church.

31Ae Sternberg Palace (Hradčany) 1698–1707
Hradčanské náměstí 15/57, Hradčany
Giovanni Battista Alliprandi

M Hradčanská

The palace cannot be seen from the square. It is
approached down a passageway from a gateway by
the archbishop's palace. When designing the palace for the Sternberg family, Alliprandi took the
designs of Viennese architect Domenico Martinelli
as a model. Although it was originally intended to
have been a much larger palace, with a wing thath
would connect it to the main square, it is actually a
simple four-wing building with a central courtyard.
Little of the exterior character of the building can be
seen, except in the elegant garden façade, which
has a two-storey rounded bay. The palace is now the
home of the National Gallery's collection of non-
Bohemian European Art, displayed on three floors.

32Bb Troja Palace 1679–85
U trojského zámku 4, Holešovice
Jean-Baptiste Mathey

M Nádraží Holešovice; B 112

The palace was built for Count Wenceslas Adalbert
of Sternberg, a high ranking official in the Czech
court, whose cosmopolitan outlook stemmed from
his extensive travels abroad. It was conceived of as
a summer chateau – an Italian villa-type – on land
that could only be reached through the royal game
reserve of Stromovka. Begun by Prague architect
Domenico Orsi and continued by his pupil Silvestro
Carloni, the palace's final character was determined by Jean-Baptiste Mathey. Following a clash
between Carloni and Mathey concerning the latter's
lack of guild membership, the count decided to
appoint Mathey as sole supervisor of the project.
Mathey's approach was to design the palace and its
formal gardens as a single entity, on an axis that
linked the palace with the distant, uninterrupted
view of Hradčany Castle.

The circular exterior staircase that marks the southern entrance is a dramatic contrast to the regular
proportions of the architecture. It is decorated with
a succession of Bernini-inspired sculptures, representing the *Struggle of the Giants*, by Dresden
sculptors Johann George and Paul Heerman.

In the centre of the building is a two-storey banquet-
ing hall, the ceiling decorated with a fresco of the
Victory of Emperor Leopold I over the Turks by
Francesco Marchetti. Marchetti was responsible for
a large part of the painted decoration, including the
chapel's oil paintings, although not all were implemented as originally planned. Faced with Marchetti's
arrogant temperament, Count Sternberg subsequently sought out other Italian painters to work on
the palace.

The palace and gardens were renovated between
1977–89, which largely restored Mathey's original
conception, and included the entire reconstruction
of the fountain to seventeenth-century designs. It is
open to the public.

An era of sumptuous display

33Ae Lobkowicz Palace (Malá Strana) 1702–4
Vlašská ul. no. 19/347, Malá Strana
Giovanni Battista Alliprandi

M Malostranská

This Lobkowicz Palace is not to be confused with
the earlier palace of the same name, which forms
part of the castle 1. The palace was built by
Alliprandi in 1702–4. It was planned with two
façades: those of the street side and the more
impressive garden front. The Lobkowicz family

acquired the palace in 1753, and it was given its
Baroque appearance by Ignaz Johann Palliardi in
1769. The building is now the German Embassy.
The garden (partly open to the public), which
stretches up Petřín Hill, was restyled in the manner of English 'natural' landscaping in 1793 by J.
Skalnik, who had been responsible for the landscaping of Marienbad Spa. The garden is dotted
with several eighteenth and nineteenth-century
structures, and is dominated by the Observation
Path, which leads up the hill to Strahov.

34Be Břevnov Abbey (Klášter a kostel sv. Markéty)
1708–45
Markétská 28/1, Břevnov
Christoph Dientzenhofer

T 8, 22

The abbey and church of St Margaret were founded
as the first (Benedictine) monastery in 993. The
crypt of the original Romanesque church remains,
but the character of the complex is entirely the work
of Christoph Dientzenhofer's rebuilding in the early
eighteenth century. The aisleless church shows how
the Baroque architect strove to create dramatic
large spaces. Christoph's work was taken over by
his son, Kilian Ignaz (who added the ornamental
gateway in 1740), although much of the monastery
and church was completed by then. The abbey was
designated a cultural monument in 1991 and
sensitive renovation work was undertaken, in anticipation of its millennium celebrations, in 1993.

35Ag Clam-Gallas Palace 1713–29

Husova 20/158, Staré Město

Johann Bernard Fischer von Erlach

Ⓜ Staroměstská

One of the more 'hidden' palaces in the Old Town, the scale and grandeur of the Clam-Gallas Palace is often missed because of its situation within these narrow streets. Johann Gallas, a top-ranking government official and ambassador to Naples, acquired the land adjoining his family property in the last decade of the seventeenth century. Johann Bernard Fischer, the Viennese imperial architect, was engaged to plan an imposing palace on the irregular site. Fischer's plan, which incorporated two courtyards, and the main façade on Husova street, was carried out by Thomas Haffenecker. Inside and out, the palace is decorated with 'muscular' sculpture, the most striking of which are Mathias Braun's giant figures which flank the entrances. Some of the exterior figures have been removed to the National Gallery, and replicas stand in their place. The palace now houses the archives of the City of Prague.

36Ae Town Houses 1720s

Nerudová 41/236 & 43/235, Malá Strana

Ⓜ Malostranská

Both of these examples of middle-class, Baroque housing, from the early eighteenth century, were adapted from earlier buildings. As in many cases, these houses retain elements of the Gothic and Renaissance buildings on the site, such as the vaulted basements, which were left when the houses were remodelled around the 1720s. Number 41 is called the House at the Red Lion and 43 the House at the Green Lobster; both take their names from the coloured relief motifs on the façades. Nerudová was becoming a fashionable street in the early eighteenth century, and most of its houses were given Baroque facelifts around the same time. Giovanni Santini-Aichl's addition of two smaller palaces in the street – the Morzin Palace and the Thun-Hohenstein Palace – between 1713 and 1726 doubtless encouraged this transformation.

An era of sumptuous display

37Bf Invalidovna House 1731–37

Sokolovská 24/136, Karlín

K. I. Dientzenhofer

M Invalidovna

The Invalidovna complex was Dientzenhofer's major secular work in Prague; a hostel for the disabled (mainly soldiers), inspired by *Les Invalides* in Paris, and commissioned by Emperor Charles VI in 1728. The land, which had been known as 'Hospital fields' since the thirteenth century, was acquired to create a complex large enough to house 4,000 patients, with facilities for their families and administration. The ground plan for the hospital was relatively simple – two central sections divided by a large central courtyard, and subdivided by smaller courtyards, three in each section. However, the scheme was never fully realised, and work halted in 1737 with only one ninth of the building completed, comprising four wings around an arcaded courtyard. The exterior of the building was adapted to create a relatively simple Neo-classical façade. The hospital now houses the Institute of Military History's archives and the National Technical Museum's archives of the history of architecture. The architectural archives contain the works of Czech architects from 1850, and are particularly rich in material relating to the first half of the twentieth century. The collections can be visited by appointment with the National Technical Museum's Department of the History of Architecture.

38Ag Kostel sv. Mikuláše (Church of St Nicholas in the Old Town) 1732–35

Staroměstské náměstí, Staré Město

K. I. Dientzenhofer

M Staroměstská

In the north-western corner of the Old Town Square is Kilian Ignaz Dientzenhofer's expressive, High Baroque domed church dedicated to St Nicholas. This church was completed shortly before the architect took over his father's work on the church of the same name in the Lesser Town **39**. Both churches demonstrate the sweeping, dynamic style that is characteristic of Kilian's work. The church site in the Old Town Square dates from the thirteenth century. By the eighteenth century it was occupied by the Benedictines. The emphasis of Kilian's new design was the south façade, with twin towers, a high portal and sculptures by Anton Braun. Inside the church, the spatial experience is heightened by the manipulation of visual effect. On the uppermost storey, miniature sculptural decoration

contributes to the impression of height. The delicate interior plasterwork is by B. Spinetti.

39Af Kostel sv. Mikuláše (Church of St Nicholas in the Lesser Town) 1703–52

Malostranské náměstí, Malá Strana

C. and K. I. Dientzenhofer

M Malostranská

The church is the centrepiece of the Lesser Town Square. It is acknowledged as one of the finest Baroque buildings in Central Europe. A church on this site, dedicated to St Nicholas, dates back to 1283. It was, for a time, the centre of Hussite rebellion. After 1625, the church was handed over to the Jesuits, who also founded their college next door. In 1703, architect Christoph Dientzenhofer was employed to create a new church, building the new nave and western frontage. After 1737, the work was continued by Dientzenhofer's son, Kilian Ignaz, who built the choir and the dome. The church and belfry tower were finally completed by Kilian's son-in-law, Anselmo Lurago, in 1755. The Dientzenhofer's creation is a complex and dynamic fusion of Baroque elements. The heavy dome contrasts with the undulating sculptural decoration in and out. The unusual vault is the result of the complex ground plan, as the placing of supporting columns creates a system of interconnecting curves.

40Ae The Loreto 1721–25

Loretánské náměstí, Hradčany

C. and K. I. Dientzenhofer

M Hradčanská; T 22

On the eastern side of Loreto Square is the Loreto complex of buildings, which were unified and extended in the eighteenth century by the Dientzenhofers. The origin of the Loreto is the legend of how the Virgin Mary's home was transferred to Italy by angels and situated in a laurel grove (hence the name, derived from Lauretum). The cult of the Loreto shrine became popular in Bohemia in the seventeenth century, and the heart of the Loreto complex is the Casa Santa, intended as a copy of the House of the Virgin Mary of Nazareth. This tiny building was the work of Giovanni Battista Orsi (1626–31) and was founded by Princess Kateřína of Lobkowicz. The buildings that grew up around the Casa Santa included the cloisters, and a series of chapels, with one in each corner of the square complex. The cloisters were extended a storey by Kilian Dientzenhofer in 1740. His father, Christoph, had begun the façade and towers in 1721; after his death, in 1722, these were completed by Kilian. The Loreto contains a treasury of precious religious artefacts.

An era of sumptuous display

41Af Kostel sv. Tomáše 1727–31

Letenská, Malá Strana

K. I. Dientzenhofer

M Malostranská

There are remains of the former Gothic basilica of the Augustine monastery on this site, dating from the late thirteenth century, and some Renaissance elements, which were built into the construction of the new church in the early eighteenth century. The fusion of old and new designs here is interesting, as Dientzenhofer respected the original plan of the church and retained what he could of the remaining building. The exterior character of the church does not really give this away. It is shoe-horned into a narrow space on the corner of the street, which surprisingly adds to the effect of Dientzenhofer's dynamic architectural language.

42Ag Goltz-Kinský Palace 1755–61

Staroměstské náměstí, Staré Město

K. I. Dientzenhofer and A. Lurago

M Staroměstská

The building of Dientzenhofer's palace for Count Johann Ernst Goltz was overseen by his son-in-law, Lurago, after Dientzenhofer's death. The cellars of the original houses have been preserved in the basement of the present building (on the north side an early Gothic house, in the west wing a Romanesque building). When the interiors were remodelled in a Neo-classical manner in the later eighteenth century, after Prince Rudolf Kinský took possession, the High Baroque façades were left intact. In 1948, the Communist leader, Gottwald, addressed the crowds prior to his coup from the balcony. More recently, the building has become the home of the National Gallery's Prints and Drawings Collection.

43Ae Archbishop's Palace 1764–65

Hradčanské náměstí 16/56, Hradčany

Johann Josef Wirch

M Hradčanská

The earlier palace on this site, built in the early sixteenth century, was acquired by the archbishop, Antonín Brus, in 1562. It had been through several rebuildings including major work by Jean-Baptiste Mathey before Wirch was given the project in the 1760s. Wirch's transformation of the palace is a good example of Rococo in Prague, which was only short-lived and was already being superseded by the Neo-classicism favoured by the empress, Maria Theresa. Wirch used Rococo decoration to enliven a Neo-classical façade, which he continued throughout the interiors. In fact, Mathey's arrangement of the façade was very little altered but the decorative character of the building was changed.

4Ag **Theatre of the Estates** 1781–83
Železná 11/540, Staré Město
Anton Haffenecker

M Staroměstská

The building of a new city theatre was financed by the Bohemian, Count Nostic-Rieneck, in an attempt to raise Prague's cultural profile. Initially, plans were drawn up for a Baroque building but were reworked in a more severe Neo-classical manner by Haffenecker. His building had four symmetrical façades, with a projecting carriage entrance on the main façade. Above the rusticated ground storey on the main façade was a window the height of the second two storeys, flanked by Corinithian columns.

The interior had two staircases accessing the theatre boxes and an auditorium with a wooden structure. In the mid nineteenth century, the theatre was remodelled inside and out. The exterior alterations included the removal of the double-height window (now two separate storeys), and the addition of the cast-iron balconies. Inside, the wooden auditorium was replaced with a a steel structure and new staircases and exits were built. These alterations, made by Achille Wolf in 1882, were mostly for reasons of safety, so that the building could be emptied more quickly. The theatre held the first performances of both opera and theatre in Czech. It gained its name when its ownership passed to the Czech Estates in 1799, but after 1945 it was also known as the Tyl Theatre, after the Czech playwright of that name.

U Hybernů House, 45

Industry and reform 1800–85

45Ah U Hybernů House 1808–11

náměstí Republicky 3/1037, Staré Město

Georg Fischer and Jan Zobel

M náměstí Republicky

At the intersection of two streets, facing the Municipal House, is this rather severe and inelegant Neoclassical Customs House: the principal example of the so-called Empire style in Prague, which borrowed from practices in both Paris and Berlin. The site was originally occupied by the church and monastery of the Irish Franciscans (or Hibernians),

built by Carlo Lurago in the 1650s. Its model was the Old Mint in Berlin (1798–1800), designed by Heinrich Gentz. Fischer, who was a professor at the Prague Technical Academy (and who had trained in Vienna), devised a plan that split the former nave into two storeys by the addition of a tunnel vault. Part of the church was demolished and the remainder converted by Zobel. Some of the monastery buildings were converted to offices. The main façade of Fischer's building is relatively unornamented, with a massive central projecting section topped by a plain cornice and attic section. The building is now used for temporary exhibitions.

46Ah Kostel sv. Kříže (Church of the Holy Cross) 1816–24

Na příkopé, Nové Město

Georg Fischer

M Můstek

This Neo-classical church was built as part of the Piarist Monastery on Pařižská Street by Fischer, shortly after he completed the nearby Customs House **45**. The church is aisleless, comprising a central space with the original interior unaltered. Like Fischer's Customs House, the church seems rather severe compared to its flamboyant Baroque counterparts. However, the buildings demonstrate both a new technical orientation to architecture (Fischer was a professor at the Technical Academy of Architecture), and the dominance of the trademark style of the Austrian empire.

Industry and reform

47Ag Platýz House 1817–25
Národní třída 37/416, Staré Město
Heinrich Hausknecht

M Národní třída

This large complex of buildings between Národní
třída and the old Coal Market (Uhelný trh) was one
of the first housing modernisation projects of the
nineteenth century, responding to the demand for
tenement dwellings in the centre of the city. The
original medieval house on the site had been extended and reconstructed prior to 1799, when it
was purchased by František Daubek with the intention of converting the site to middle-class tenement
housing. On his advice, Hausknecht built the wing
facing Národní třída in a Neo-classical style, and
unified the whole complex with an Empire face-lift.
The new buildings had accommodation for private
residences as well as rooms for trade and entertaining.

The apartments surround a large public courtyard
with entrances at either end and accessed by five
staircases. Platýz became a model for the tenement
housing boom in the 1830s and 1840s.

The complex was rebuilt in the 1930s by František
Krasny, who modernised the ground floor shops
and added a glass roofed arcade to the courtyard.

48Bf The development of Karlín 1817–
Karlínské náměstí and environs, Karlín

M Křížíkova

The enlightened planning regulations of 1817 ush-
ered in a new period of building control in Prague.
The development of the suburb of Karlín was the
first example of this, comprising a grid-plan of
broad avenues transversed with narrower residential streets, and parks and gardens. The suburb was
entered from the city at Poříčská Gate (Na Poříčí).
It still retains many of the standardised Neo-classical apartment blocks, as well as some later *fin-de-
siècle* housing. The local industry of Karlín included
a textile factory, steam engine works and the Prague
Gasworks, built in 1847. An electric tram system

was installed in 1895. The suburb had its own town
hall, the Municipal House **96**, and a school (1906).
The Church of Sts Cyril and Methodius in the central
square was designed by Karl Rösner and Ignác Ullmann
between 1854 and 1863, in a Neo-Romanesque style.

49Ai Kinský Villa and Gardens 1827–31
náměstí Kinskych, Smichov
Heinrich Koch

M Anděl; T 9, 12

The park on the edge of Petřín Hill was established
by the Czech patriot, Count Rudolf Kinský and
modelled on eighteenth-century English landscaping traditions by Franz Höhnel in 1825. Shortly
after, Kinský added the Neo-classical garden villa,
designed by Viennese architect Koch. The villa is
built on a terrace, due to the slope of the hill, and is
a storey higher on the east side. The porticoed east
entrance has a gallery above, with ornamental
railings. On the western façade is the carriage
entrance, with a double height portico. At the

southern end of the building is a winter garden
room, on the ground floor, which is lit by five large
windows. The building was decorated with sculptures by Antonio Canova and Emanuel Max. It now
houses the Ethnographic Museum and a collection
of vernacular furniture and Folk decorative arts,
mostly from the ethnographic exhibitions of 1891

and 1895. It is in a bad state of repair and does not appear to be open to the public. The park's original character is not very obvious, as subsequent remodelling added new waterways, fountains and

rare plants. There are two other buildings by Koch in the grounds: a service building in the lower grounds, built in 1829, and a glass house of the same date on the higher slopes.

50Ab Klár Institute for the Blind 1836–44

Klárov 6/131, Malá Straná

Vincenc Kulhánek

M Malostranská

The Klár Institute was founded by Professor Alois Klár and built by his son in the spirit of nineteenth-century philanthropy and medical reform. The Neo-classical façade, with its central clock tower and projecting central section, was designed by Kulhánek and is decorated by a frieze in the pediment by Josef Max. The Chapel of St Raphael, which is attached to the building, was designed at the same time by Josef Kranner and decorated with frescoes by leading Czech artists.

51Ah Masarykovo nádraží (Masaryk Station) 1842–45

Hybernska 13/1014, Nové Město

Antonín Jungling

M náměstí Republicky

The Masaryk (or Central) station is Prague's oldest railway station, constructed to receive trains from Vienna via Olomouc on the new rail system built by the Austrian Empire. The new station was planned as one of Europe's largest and most impressive. It was ceremonially opened on 20 August 1845. The city's chief engineer, Antonín Jungling, constructed two buildings on Hybernská and Havlíckova streets. The first, for departures, is a twin towered building

with a large station hall containing booking offices, waiting rooms and a post office. The second, for arrivals, is a large, glass-roofed hall. In 1866, another two-storey restaurant building was constructed at the corner of the two streets between the existing buildings, and the platforms' cast-iron roofing system was extended. The building was restored to its original Neo-classical appearance in the mid 1980s. The original construction and architectural detail is now fully visible. Although the whole project was masterminded by Jungling, there is some debate as to whether he was the author of the architectural conception. The Viennese Court architects Paul Sprenger and Peter de Nobile, who were working in Prague at the time, have also been linked with the project.

Industry and reform

52Ag Emperor Franz I Memorial 1844–46

Smetanovo nábřeží, Staré Město

Josef Kranner

M Staroměstská

In 1841, the Provincial Diet ordered the purchase of the buildings and land along this section of the river bank, which was a frequent site of dangerous flooding. Along the edge of the river an embankment was constructed (the first in the city), designed by Bernard Grueber and the city construction office, and built of large granite blocks. Behind the wide avenue, two Neo-classical apartment blocks were built, surrounding a small park, one of the first attempts at uniform planning in the city. In the centre of the little park is this Neo-Gothic memorial to Emperor Francis I, made by sculptor Karel Svoboda to the designs of Kranner. It is a Gothic tower surrounded by allegorical figures representing the crafts and trades of Prague, rather like the later Albert Memorial in London. A bronze statue of the emperor, seated on a horse, was placed in the centre of the tower, but has since been removed to the Lapidarum Museum **64**.

53Ak Lažansky Palace 1861–63

Smetanovo nábřeží, Staré Město

Ignác V. Ullmann

M Narodní třída

Ullmann was one of the first architects to use Renaissance models for private houses and public buildings in Prague, borrowing from both French and Italian models. At the south end of the new embankment, he built this four-storey palace for Count Lažansky in the style of the French Renaissance, with a mansard roof and corner roof turrets. The building was extended to the west in 1894 by Franz Schachner, who stayed faithful to Ullmann's original design.

The palace contained a number of luxurious, upper-class apartments. The composer, Smetana, lived in one for a few years in the 1860s, when he wrote the opera *The Bartered Bride*. On the lower floor of the palace is the elegant Café Slavia and the wine bar, Parnas. The café interiors were designed in the 1930s by Oldřich Stefan, when it became a favourite hangout of artists and writers (and later an important meeting place for the underground movement in the 1960s and 1970s). After the revolution of 1989, the Slavia was closed for several years, supposedly for restoration by its new commercial owners. This caused some protest from the artistic community, who see it as a part of their recent history. It reopened in 1998, with minor alterations and a rather bland interior design. A new cocktail bar, complete with Starck lights, has been added.

54Ap Provincial Maternity Hospital 1867–75

Apolinářská 18/441, Nové Město

Josef Hlávka

M náměstí I. P. Pavlova

Changing attitudes to public welfare, as well as a new economic prosperity, encouraged the patronage of new health care institutions in the second half of the nineteenth century. Hlávka's design for the Maternity Hospital was considered to be both progressive and appropriate to the needs of patients and medical staff. The plan consists of six parallel wings connected to the main body of the building by two corridors, which form a central courtyard with the northern entrance wing. This wing contains administrative space as well as a small chapel, decorated with wall paintings (however, access is virtually impossible). The wards are located in the south facing outer wings and the delivery rooms in the central corridors. The building is designed in an English Neo-Gothic style, with polychromatic brickwork and stone window tracery, as well as stepped gabling. Although it is still used as a hospital, the building is in a bad state of repair.

55Ag Spanish Synagogue 1868–93

Vězeňská 1, Josefov

Ignác V. Ullmann and Josef Niklas

M Staroměstská

This little synagogue is the most modern of the Josefov synagogues. It is designed in a Moorish style, on the foundations of a twelfth-century synagogue. Its style was certainly characteristic of nineteenth-century European orientalism, although this was not very common in Prague. In fact, its name came from the community of Spanish Jews, who had settled in the city in the fifteenth century, after fleeing the Spanish Inquisition. The older building on this site, despite modernisations, became so inadequate that it was completely demolished in the 1860s. Ullmann's new building drew from the origins of the synagogue, and Niklas provided interior decoration based upon the Alhambra. The synagogue cannot be viewed inside, as it now acts as a storehouse for the Jewish Museum's collection of textiles. Another exotic Moorish design was used for the 1906 Jubilee synagogue, which was built in the New Town.

Industry and reform

56Bh New Provost's Lodgings and Deanery 1872–77
K Rotundě 4/89 & 10/100, Vyšehrad
Josef Niklas

M Vyšehrad; T 18, 24

During the second half of the nineteenth century, the Vyšehrad castle area became a focus for the Czech national revival, which led to a certain amount of rebuilding in a national-historicist style. The Provost's Lodging House is a Neo-Gothic residence, which now serves as a hall for weddings and concerts. Inside, the chapel, now used for wedding ceremonies, is highly decorated with paintings of Czech patron saints, and has an oriel window facing onto the street. Several canons' houses next door were also built by Niklas, in the same style. The old deanery now contains an exhibition on the history of Vyšehrad.

57Bh Kostel sv. Petra a Pavla (Church of Sts Peter and Paul) 1885–87
Vyšehrad
Josef Mocker

M Vyšehrad; T 18, 24

The church, on the Vyšehrad Castle site 2, dates back to the eleventh century, but its present exterior appearance is almost entirely the result of its Gothic Revival reconstruction in the 1880s. Mocker removed many Baroque features from the church and decorated the interior with rich polychromatic designs. The Baroque façade of the church was at first left alone, but replaced with a Gothic façade with two slim steeples in 1902–3 by Mocker and his colleague, František Mikš. The portal is decorated with a relief depicting the *Last Judgement*. Close by, the new façade appears oversized in relation to the nave of the church, but the blackened Gothic towers can be seen for miles around, and suit the Romantic image of Vyšehrad.

Next to the church is the National Cemetery, which was planned on the site of an old graveyard. It is where many prominent Czech figures associated with the National Revival movement are buried. Many of the monuments were designed by Antonín Barvitius and Antonín Wiehl, including the Slavín, or Pantheon (a common tomb for Czech heroes), which was built in 1889–93. On the northern side of the cemetery are some arcades, designed by Wiehl in 1902. Within the arcades are several Art Nouveau memorials, each of them very distinctive. It is worth spending time here to search out names: the composers Smetana and Dvořák, writers Karel Čapek and Mikoláš Aleš, the painter Alfons Mucha and sculptors Jan Štursa, Josef Václav Myslbek and Ladislav Šaloun. The architects buried here include Josef Gočár and Jaroslav Fragner.

58Ak   National Theatre 1868–83

Národní 2/223, Staré Město

Josef Zítek and Josef Schulz

M Národní třída

The project to build the new National Theatre was one of the clearest assertions of national pride and the concern for a national style at this time. Originally built to a plan of Zítek's in 1881, the theatre was paid for largely with monies raised through a national collection. However, in August 1881, the theatre burnt down, scarcely a month after its official opening. It was reconstructed by Zítek's pupil, Josef Schulz, according to the original design. This time, the restoration was paid for by the city and the Austrian emperor. Schulz also reconstructed the adjacent Provisionary Theatre (originally built in 1862 by Ullmann), and added an additional wing that connects the two buildings, forming a whole.

The Neo-Renaissance building shows the interest in Italian architecture on the part of both architects.

Schulz had spent two extensive periods in Italy, funded by a government research grant. The building is decorated with reliefs and sculpture depicting allegorical figures (the Muses and Apollo on the uppermost storey of the loggia). Most of the decoration, both internal and external, depicts symbols of the dramatic arts, and of national history. The decoration of the building was completed by a range of leading Czech artists. The bronze figure of the Goddess of Victory (1910–11) on the main façade by the artists F. Rous, E. Halman and Šaloun, was the subject of Schulz's opposition.

59AI   National Museum 1885–91

Vaclavksé náměstí 68/1700, Nové Město

Josef Schulz

M Muzeum

Originally founded as the Patriotic Museum of the Kingdom of Bohemia in 1818, and housed in various temporary sites in the city, the National Museum was granted a site for its first purpose-built accommodation in 1876. This was finally decided in an architectural competition of 1883. Six prominent architects participated, including Antonín Wiehl, but the commission was finally awarded to Schulz. What was significant about Schulz's design, in preference to the others and as a suitable expression of national concerns, was his inclusion of a grand domed Pantheon, intended for ceremonial occasions. The Pantheon extends through all floors of the building, with a vaulted dome and high cupola. It is decorated with wall paintings, the largest of which are by František Zenisek.

The museum dominates Wenceslas Square, and provides a grand and ceremonial access to the top of the square from its staircase. However, the redesign of the traffic system around the top of the square has left the museum stranded on its own island, making access difficult for the visitor.

60Ag Rudolfinum (House of the Artists) 1876–84
námēstí Jana Palacha 1/79, Staré Mēsto
Josef Zítek and Josef Schulz

M Staromēstská

Conceived as a 'temple to the arts', and paid for with funds provided by the Bohemian Savings Bank (to mark their fiftieth anniversary), the Rudolfinum is the most important example of Czech Neo-Renaissance after the National Theatre **58**. The architects won the competition in 1874 to design a building to house a concert hall, music conservatory, picture gallery and museum of applied arts. The competition for the building's decoration called for works that depicted the history of the Bohemian arts, and

attracted submissions from all over Central Europe. Graduates of the major European Schools of design were employed on the decoration of the building, including the sculpture on the attic storey, which depicts leading composers and visual artists. The consultation team for the project included the composer, Richard Wagner. The interior of the Dvořák concert hall was based on the theatre at Versailles. During the First Czech Republic (1918–38), and briefly after the war, the Rudolfinum housed the National Parliament. Since 1989, the building has gradually been restored to its original use, and is now the home of the Czech Philharmonic, and an exhibition venue and café. (Jan Palach Square was previously named Red Army Square, and renamed in 1990 after one of the heroes of the Prague Spring.)

61Ag School of Applied Arts 1881–84
námēstí Jana Palacha 3/80, Staré Mēsto
František Schmoranz and Jan Machytka

M Staromēstská

This four-storey building was constructed as part of the monumental redesign of the riverside, which followed the building of a footbridge to the Lesser Quarter. The building became the School of Decorative Arts in 1995. It is built in a Neo-Renaissance style like its more impressive counterpart, the Rudolfinum **60**, opposite. The façade facing the Rudolfinum is rusticated on the lower two storeys, and the upper two storeys have large windows to light the studios. The sculptural decoration

of the exterior is largely replica work (including copies of Michelangelo's *Night* and *Day*). There is also a bust of Jan Kotēra (of 1924), who was professor of the School of Architecture from 1898–1910.

62AI Church of St Ludmilla 1888–93
náměstí Míru, Nové Město
Josef Mocker

M náměstí Míru

Mocker's brand of brick architecture is demonstrated to good effect in this church. Mocker was known for his restoration work on medieval religious buildings, as well as for his attempts to promote a Neo-Gothic National Style. This triple-naved church is a pared-down version of that style, designed with a severity and little of the delicacy of, for example, Mocker's work on the Cathedral of St Vitus. The principal exterior decorative feature is the tympanum on the main doorway by another great national artist, Myslbek. Inside the church, the severity is enlivened by polychromatic decoration on the walls and vaults, and a dramatic stained glass window.

Industrial Palace, 1891, 65

The path to nationhood 1890–1918

63Ag **The Redevelopment of Josefov** 1893 onwards

Staré Město

Planned by Alfred Hurtig and Josef Sakař

M Staroměstská

The modernisation of Prague from the 1890s onwards was to embrace all aspects of life: political, economic, social, cultural, intellectual and aesthetic. The demographic expansion of the city, coupled with an increasing prosperity in some sections of society encouraged plans to redesign and rebuild certain regions of the city. First to be targeted was the old Jewish ghetto – at this point in a poor and insanitary state. This ruthless replanning of the area, proposed by Hurtig and his colleagues, following a competition in 1893, involved the destruction of all but a few key Jewish monuments. The newly named Josefov was to be based on a grid plan, with Pařížská Street as its main axis. This main boulevard was an attempt to bring to Prague some of the grandiose scale of Hausmann's Paris – a far cry from the city's medieval street plan. Like Paris, the replanning of Prague also provided the opportunity for social reorganisation; as the displaced poor moved out to the lesser suburbs, so the fashionable bourgeoisie moved in. The other major existing roads around Pařížská – Dušni, Siroká, Maiselova, Kaprova and Josefovská – were widened. In between these major carriageways were smaller streets and apartment blocks with rather cramped courtyards. Hurtig's plan was given form by another

competition for the architectural character of Josefov in 1893. The winner, Josef Sakař, applied a vision more picturesque than rationalistic to Hurtig's original conception. The apartment blocks in Josefov are mostly in the fashionable Neo-Baroque or Neo-Renaissance style of the time. Others indicate more clearly the direction of Art Nouveau. With the opening of new shops, bars and galleries, Pařížská is once again one of the most fashionable streets in Prague. Individual apartment buildings include:

Bílkova 13–15/884 1905 *František Velich.*
Kaprova 5/19, 1904 *Jiří Stribal.*
Kaprova, 6/52, 1906 *Bedřich Bendelmayer.*
Pařížská 1/1073, 1901–2 *Jan Koula.*
Pařížská 16/125, 1905–6 *Matěj Blecha.*
Siroká 9/96, 1908 *Karel Mašek.*
Žatecká 5/18, 1900 *Jiří Stribal.*
Žatecká 2/110, 1914–15 *Josip Plečnik, Ladislav Skřivánek and Stanislav Vávra.*

64Bb **Site of the Jubilee Exhibition** 1891

U Výstaviště, Bubeneč

Antonín Wiehl

M Nadrazi Holešovice; T 5, 12, 17

The organisation of the Regional Jubilee Exhibition in 1891 gave architects the opportunity to experiment with new constructional techniques and industrial materials. This exhibition and its successor, the Ethnographic Exhibition of 1895, also provided an architectural rallying point for the emerging national movement. Architects explored various means of national expression through design, employing a range of historicist and vernacular forms. Like the other grand expositions of the modern age in Europe and America, the 1891 exhibition gave the Czechs the chance to proclaim their modernity.

The path to nationhood

The site, on a corner of the old Deer Park, was laid out according to the plans made by the city architect, Antonín Wiehl. The team of architects employed to design the exhibition pavilions utilised Wiehl's favoured Bohemian Historicist styles, as well as the engineering skills of the First Bohemian Steelworks. The wooden structures, including the turreted gateway, have since been pulled down. One of the pavilions to attract most attention was Wiehl's Bohemian Cottage – this interest in vernacular traditions was the main impetus behind the organisation of the Ethnographic Exhibition four years later. This was followed by a succession of trade and cultural exhibitions. Other Pavilions were added and existing ones remodelled in subsequent years. In front of the Industrial Palace are two smaller pavilions. The Prague Pavilion, designed by Antonín Wiehl in 1891, was remodelled several years later by Antonín Hrubý. It now houses the City of Prague's Lapidarium; a collection of architectural artefacts and sculpture. The updated building is decorated with reliefs by Gustav Zoula representing events from Bohemian history. It originally had sculpted allegorical figures in the entrance by František Hergesel, which have been removed and are now inside. Opposite, the Panorama Pavilion was designed by Jan Koula to house the panoramic scene of the 1494 Battle of Lipany, painted by Luděk Marold, among others, in 1898.

In addition to its revivalist tendencies, the 1891 exhibition provided a model of innovation and modernity, show-casing the widespread architectural use of industrial materials such as iron and glass, as well as the installation of an electricity network that supplied, among other things, the famous light fountains (designed by František Krizik) and the telephone system. The transport and tram networks were extended to embrace the new site, and the exhibition promoted the residential development of this suburb of Prague.

Although some pavilions from the 1890s were only temporary, much of the original site remains. In the 1950s, the park was renamed the Julius Fucik Park of Culture and Rest, after the Communist hero, and the name changed again in the 1980s, and in 1991 Výstaviště was again the site for a centenary exhibition of trade and culture when a number of new structures were added 181.

65Bb **Industrial Palace** 1891

U Výstaviště, Bubeneč

Bedřich Münzberger and František Prášil

M Nadrazi Holešovice; T 5, 12, 17

(Illustration page 72) Originally built for the Jubilee Exhibition of 1891, the Industrial Palace was one of the first large scale constructions of iron and glass in Prague. Münzberger added the Neo-Baroque features to the frame of the building, designed by the engineer, František Prášil, with the First Bohemian Steelworks. The palace exemplifies how architects tried to reconcile the desire for a strong decorative identity with modern developments in engineering. With the new constructional possibilities, the architect's role had to be quickly redefined. The exhibition architecture of the *fin de siècle* represents this transitional period in the development of Modernism, because it seems to pull in two directions. In Prague, as in other cities, questions of national identity expressed through architectural style took precedence over the complete exploitation of the engineer's new skills.

Münzberger's original design for the interiors was modified in 1907 by Josef Fanta, with further structural alterations made in 1952–54 by Pavel Smetana. For the centenary celebrations of 1991, further structures were added 181.

66Ab **Hanavský Pavilion** 1891
Letná Plain
Otto Hieser
M Hradčanská

Originally built as part of the 1891 Jubilee Exhibition, the pavilion was transferred to its present site on Letná Plain in 1898, where it now houses a café. The building was assembled from cast-iron parts made at the Prince of Hanau Ironworks, and was therefore something of a technical achievement, serving as a giant advertisement for the company's products. Like the majority of exhibition buildings, it was designed in a flamboyant Neo-Baroque style, but also exploits the design possibilities of an industrial material.

67Ae **Petřín Tower** 1891
Petřín Hill
František Prášil
M Újezd

The engineer responsible for the Industrial Palace at the 1891 Jubilee Exhibition also built this lookout tower for the same celebrations. Intended as a mini-Eiffel Tower (although the experience is more Blackpool than Paris), it stands 60 metres high and can still be reached by the Újezd funicular railway built at the same time. The addition of two funiculars and the extension of tram lines connected several exhibition sites across the city.

68Ag **Czech National Savings Bank** 1892–94
Rytířská 29/536, Staré Město
Antonín Wiehl and Osvald Polívka
M Müstek

The economic boom in Bohemia at the end of the nineteenth century resulted in the rapid expansion of the banking and insurance system in Prague. Banks demanded prestigious premises in the city centre, rather like Renaissance princes building their city palaces. Capitalising on the popularity of National Style architecture, the banks acted as patrons to artists and architects working in this manner. Wiehl and Polívka's building for the former City Savings Bank occupies a site in the old market, adjacent to Havelské Square. Construction was by the influential developer, Quido Bělský, and the sculptural decoration was by a range of notable Czech artists, including Stanislav Sucharda. Inside,

The path to nationhood

there is a central staircase leading to the first-floor Banking Hall. Originally the Banking Hall was lit from above, but an extra storey was added to the building much later. The interiors are decorated with paintings and elaborate stucco work, some from cartoons by the national artist, Mikoláš Aleš. Alterations were made to the building in the 1950s, when it was converted according to plans made by Jan Zázvorka to house the Klement Gottwald Museum, dedicated to the worker's revolutionary movement in Czechoslovakia and to the (later discredited) Communist leader. The building continues to house temporary exhibitions of various types on the ground floor, and its interiors are therefore generally accessible.

69AI Wiehl's House 1894–96

Vodičkova 40/792, Nové Město

Antonín Wiehl and Josef Fanta

M Müstek

This five-storey building on the corner of Vodičkova and Vaclavské náměstí was designed by city architect Wiehl, with the assistance of Fanta, in his characteristic Bohemian Neo-Renaissance style. The use of figurative sgraffitto and painted decoration, together with ornate gabling and turrets was drawn from sixteenth-century Bohemian architecture. The figurative work derives from ethnographic motifs and was, in part, designed by the artist, Mikoláš Aleš. Wiehl's attempt at a National Style had a political agenda, as it harked back to the period before the loss of Czech independence in 1620 and was geographically specific. It found favour with the national movement, but in turn this was effaced both stylistically and politically by a more progressive and forward looking generation. Although this particular example is historicist, other examples of buildings from this period tend to blend revivalist forms with an emergent modern style.

70Ah Zemská Bank 1894–96

Na příkopě 20/858, Staré Město

Osvald Polívka

M Müstek

Polívka was one of the highly successful architects of this generation to employ an eclectic range of styles. The Zemská Bank is determinably Bohemian – designed in the Neo-Renaissance style pioneered by Josef Zítek (Polívka's former teacher) and Antonín Wiehl. This bank is Romantic and extravagant both inside and out, decorated with references to Bohemian myth and allegory, as well as botanical motifs. Inside are murals and sculptures by leading Czech artists, including Stanislav Sucharda and Antonín Procházka. The two *Work* murals near the entrance are by Maximilián Švabinský. The Banking Hall is on the first floor as is common in Czech banks, and is decorated with a series of twelve sculpted figures, each representing a different region of Bohemia. The fountain in the centre is by Ladislav Šaloun.

71Bb   **Villa Koula** 1895–96
Slavíčkova 17/153, Bubeneč
Jan Koula

M Hradčanská

Influenced by the Ethnographic Exhibition of 1895, Koula employed a Romantic vernacular for his own house in the wealthy garden suburb of Bubeneč. The planning of the garden villa between roughly 1895 and 1910 shows architects tussling with the rationalisation of domestic space. This small collection of houses **78**, **88**, **89** demonstrates this development. Whereas the work of the architect in the urban centre was often concerned only with the façade – the planning of tenements being largely determined by the site or the client – middle-class homes gave them the opportunity to take up lessons learnt from England and the work of Morris, Webb and Voysey. Koula's home, with its garden aspect, shows the arrangement of the service elements of the house on the street side. His picturesque style echoes that of his teacher, Antonín Wiehl, and the drive to exploit vernacular forms.

72Ag   **Bohemian Eagle Building** 1896–97
Ovocný trh 15, Staré Město
Friedrich Ohnmann

M náměstí Republicky

This apartment and retail building is another example of Ohnmann's flamboyant reinterpretation of Czech Renaissance and Baroque architecture. The painted façade seen here became a key feature of both Revivalist and Art Nouveau buildings at the turn of the century. Ohnmann rather jokily 'draws' brickwork onto the façades, and eclectically adds details borrowed from the vernacular revival. It is, in this sense, a most transitional building – within a year he was working in the spirit of Art Nouveau. The second façade of the building can be seen at Celetná **30**.

The path to nationhood

73Bf   Museum of the City of Prague 1896–1902
Na poříčí 52/1554, Nové Město
Antonín Balšánek

M Florenc

The city museum was set up to document the
development of the city, and contains many interesting exhibits that detail its architecture, planning
and social history, such as Antonín Langweil's
model of the city, dating from the 1830s. After the
foundation of the museum in 1874, the collections
were displayed in the Šverma Park pavilion café
nearby until the permanent building was erected.
Balšánek's Neo-Renaissance building was based
on initial drawings made by Antonín Wiehl. The two-
storey building is comprised of a central entrance
section, where the grandiose circular staircase is
situated, and two side wings each containing four
exhibition halls. The building is decorated with
allegorical references to the city and its history.

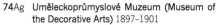

**74Ag   Uměleckoprůmyslové Muzeum (Museum of
the Decorative Arts)** 1897–1901
ul. 17. Listopadu 2, Josefov
Josef Schulz

M Staroměstská

Like many of Central Europe's decorative arts museums, the UPM was inspired by the founding
principles of the South Kensington Museum (now
the Victoria & Albert Museum) in London. Exhibitions devoted to contemporary crafts and manufac-
tures had been organised by the Prague Chamber
of Commerce since the 1860s, and Czech representatives had participated in the World Fairs since
1867. Objects purchased from subsequent exhibitions went on to form the basis of the museum's
collection when it was founded in 1885, situated in
the Rudolfinum House of Artists **60**. Monies donated
by the Chamber of Commerce, the municipality and
the Austrian government went towards a purpose-
built museum, construction of which began in
1897. Once the new building was established, the
museum continued with its mission of raising standards in manufacture and public taste.

The museum was one of the first important public
buildings to be erected on the newly cleared site of
the Jewish town, but was not eventually incorporated into the planning of the new quarter – it faces
away from Josefov, with its back to the remaining
Jewish cemetery. Instead, the Neo-Renaisssance
style of the museum relates it to the family of Czech
National Style public monuments (like the National Theatre **58** and National Museum **59**), rather

than the emergent style of Art Nouveau which
characterised Josefov from 1900 onwards. The
museum has three storeys, containing permanent
and temporary exhibition spaces, and a library with
reading room. The impressive staircase leading
from the entrance is richly decorated with allegorical paintings by František Herčik and Karel Vítězslav,
and stained glass designed by Schulz himself. The
exterior of the building is decorated with reliefs
depicting the various crafts by such artists as
Bohuslav Schnirch and Antonín Popp. In the basement of the museum is a stylish new café, designed
by architects Libor Habanec and Michal Hobza in
1991, and furnished by the Czech independent
wing of the Thonet company.

75Ag **Peterkuv Dům (Peterka House)** 1899–1900
Václavské náměstí 12/72, Nové Město
Jan Kotěra

M Můstek

This was the first building in Prague designed by
Kotěra, and demonstrates his rejection of the currently popular historical eclecticism in favour of a
unifying principle of design. The façade is decorated with Secessionist Style motifs – much plainer
and more geometric that the excessive vegetable
and floral decoration of other Art Nouveau façades.
The use of ornament is restrained and the structure
and form of the building is clearly and unequivo-
cally expressed. The decorative elements above
each side arch are flattened and abstracted, in
contrast to the figural decoration below the roofline.
Kotěra's modern style had its roots in Viennese
Secessionist design, particularly the work of Otto
Wagner.

76Ah **Hotel Central** 1898–1900
Hybernská 10
*Friedrich Ohnmann, Alois Dryak and Bedřich
Bendelmayer*

M náměstí Republicky

Begun by Ohnmann and finished by his pupils, the
Hotel Central was the precursor to the more exuber-
ant Europa Hotel **82** on Vaclavské náměstí. It is also
one of the earliest Art Nouveau buildings still surviving in the city. In 1897, Ohnmann had been responsible for the fashionable Café Corso, thought of as
the first design to completely embrace 'true' Art
Nouveau principles and totally reject historicism.
The café has since been demolished, so the Hotel
Central, Ohnmann's next project, must be considered in its place. The regular façade of the hotel is
decorated with a tree motif that continues up past
the glass canopy below the roof gable. Sadly, the Art
Nouveau interiors designed by the architects have
been removed, but the façade has recently been
refurbished.

The path to nationhood

77Ag Prague City Savings Bank 1899–1901
Staroměstské náměstí 6/932, Staré Město
Osvald Polívka

M Staroměstská

This is another of Polívka's extravagant and eclectic bank commissions, this time exploiting the wedding-cake Baroque of the surrounding Old Town Square. Polívka's success with commercial commissions such as these must have been due to his ability to work confidently in a number of styles, maintaining an awareness of historical surroundings but allowing often humorous concessions to the modern nature of his buildings. On this insurance building, the classical figures on the roof are replaced in one corner by a fireman brandishing a hose. The use of colourful decoration, such as the mural set into the façade, is something of a trademark of Polívka's buildings. The rear façade of the building (Salvátorská 6) is a more restrained attempt at Art Nouveau. Its 'modernity' pales in comparison to its later neighbour, the wonderful Štenc House **93**.

78Bb Villa Mašek 1901
Slavíčkova 7/196, Bubeneč
Karel Vítěszlav Mašek

M Hradčanská

Mašek was a painter and graphic artist, a rival of Alfons Mucha, who worked in Paris and Prague. He designed this villa for himself and family as a *Gesamtkunstwerk* ('total work of art'), combining historicist and naturalistic references in the decoration inside and out. Mašek's development of an artistic language based on nature, allowing him to gradually abandon historicism, is typical of the period. He argued that the study of nature allowed for the expression of true subjectivity. Next door to Mašek's house is another artist's villa, designed by Gustav Papež, in 1899–1900, which demonstrates a similar use of the vernacular and organic decoration (Slavíčkova 9/173).

Slavíčkova 9/173

79AI Novák Building 1901–4

Vodičkova 30/699, Nové Město

Osvald Polívka

M Müstek

This building marks Polívka's most decisive shift from historicist styles to Art Nouveau. His preference for working with artists is evident – almost the whole of the façade has been turned into a canvas for artist Jan Preisler's *Spring* and *Trade and Industry* murals. The design of the building is quite standard, and enlivened with Art Nouveau ironwork and a magnificent stained-glass entrance. Originally a department store, the building was based upon Parisian models, with a central sales hall two storeys high.

80AI Hlavní nádraží (Central Station) 1901–9

Wilsonova 2/300, Vinohrady

Josef Fanta

M Hlavní nádraží

Prague's new main station at the beginning of this century was designed in a way that tried to reconcile the modern and the historic. The section at the front of the station, which contains the ticket halls and cafés, only partly conceals the two giant glass and steel structures covering the platforms behind. The front station building has a central hall with a vaulted roof and a large semi-circular window above the main entrance. On either side of the entrance are stone towers with round glass cupolas. The towers and the façade balconies are all supported by sculpted figures by leading Art Nouveau artists, including Stanislav Sucharda. The rest of the decoration is a combination of geometric and figurative work on stucco, with sections of the façade left as plain brick. Inside the entrance are cavernous halls leading to richly decorated restaurant rooms, with tiled and painted sections and, in places, the original light fittings. The integrated use of decoration, and the endless repetition of key motifs throughout the building, is probably Fanta's greatest achievement here.

The recent redesign of the station means it is possible to enter the station at a lower level and miss much of this. Fanta's grand building has been partly effaced by the addition of a new departure hall, built in front of the main façade in 1980. The redevelopment of the station, however, did make efforts to protect the interior qualities of Fanta's plan. Station users now approach the station through the new hall, which leads them under Wilsonova to emerge in the main building. The new three-level building, with its glazed towers and roof-top carpark, was designed by J. Danda. It also contains the Metro C-line station by J. Trnka.

The path to nationhood

81 Bf Vinohrady Market Hall 1902
Vinohradská 50/1200, Vinohrady
Antonín Turek

M náměstí Míru

This Neo-Renaissance market hall served its original function as a produce market until fairly recently. It has since been converted to a more
upmarket retail centre, with cafés and fashion
stores. The three-storeyed hall is positioned on the
slope between Vinohradská and Slezská, so that
you enter the building at lower-ground rather than
ground-floor level from Vinohradská. There is a
further basement level which was originally used for
cold storage. The main hall of the building has a
cast-iron walkway at first floor level, now with shop
units along it. The conversion is rather unsympa-
thetic, using materials and finishes that do little to
complement the remaining decorative and structural ironwork inside. Several of this style of market
hall were constructed in the districts of Prague at
the turn of the century.

82 Al Europa Hotel 1903–7
Václavské náměstí, no. 25/826, Nové Město
Alois Dryák and Bedřich Bendelmayer

M Müstek

The hotel and interiors were designed by two of
Ohnmann's pupils, continuing their partnership after
the 1900 Hotel Central **76**. The Europa was originally
two adjoining hotels, the Archduke Štěpán and the
smaller Hotel Garni. It is now one of the most popular
architectural attractions in the city. The asymmetrical
façade is decorated with naturalistic ornament, with
swags and wreaths that are carried into the interior
decoration. The decorative metalwork and the mosaic show the use of a more abstracted language,
including flattened and geometric forms.

The interiors are among the most impressive Art
Nouveau examples remaining (and accessible) in
Prague. The main café on the ground floor is
panelled with a gallery, and was undoubtedly influenced by Jan Kotěra and his Vienna Secession
connections. This and the upstairs café rank with
the finest surviving interiors from this period found
anywhere in Europe. Details such as the painted
panels inset into the straightbacked booths and the
detailed ornate ironwork are reminiscent of the
work of the Glasgow Four. However, the concessions
to opulence and the hotel's wealthy clientele are
apparent too, for there is none of the control and
severity of later modern interiors.

83Ah Apartment Building 1903–4

U Prašné brány 1/1078, 3/1079, Staré Město

Bedřich Bendelmayer

M náměstí Republicky

Bendelmayer began this apartment block, situated close to the medieval Powder Tower, while work continued on the Hotel Europa in Vaclavské náměstí. Compared to the majority of apartment blocks erected during this current building boom, Bendelmayer's building is starkly plain – his use of decoration is limited to strips of geometric pattern and infrequently repeated relief panels. The curved street corner of the building is topped by a glass-walled studio room that provoked an angry response from the architectural press. One of the more conservative critics of the time, František Harlas, chose Bendelmayer's building as the focal point for an attack upon modern architecture – 'the glass house look' – in Prague, declaring the building to be incompatible with its historic neighbours.

84Ak Hlahol Choir Building 1903–6

Masarykovo nábřeží 16/248, Nové Město

Josef Fanta

M Narodní třída

Fanta's office and apartment building for the Hlahol Choir Association combines the restrained use of Secessionist detailing with a more classical use of sculptural decoration, by Josef Pekárek. The building form – a central section with curved gable flanked by two taller, narrower towers – was becoming a common building type in Prague, and had been borrowed from Otto Wagner. The colourful mosaic in the gable represents *Music*, and there are other musical motifs on the façade. Above one doorway is a mosaic, *Phoenix*. The bright and fresh decoration on the front of the building reflects an interest among some architects in the Prague tradition of the painted façade – another exceptional example of this is Polívka's Novak Building 79. In the interests of modernity, Fanta apparently tried to create an integrated building and interior, but the latter is inaccessible, so this cannot be confirmed.

It is worth comparing the Hlahol building to another by Fanta that is nearby: the **Hlávka Students' Hostel** (1903–4), at Jenštejnská 1/1966. The hostel was commissioned by the founder of the Czech academy of Arts and Sciences, J. Hlávka, and served as a Communist interrogation centre in the 1970s. It is now a hotel.

The path to nationhood

'Praha' Insurance Company building

85Ak   Topič Publishing House 1905–8

Národní 9/1010, Staré Město

Osvald Polívka

M Národní třída

This was designed as premises for the publisher, František Topič, at the same time as Polívka was working on the adjacent **'Praha' Insurance Company building** (Národní 7/1011). These two buildings show Polívka incorporating elements of Art Nouveau with classical and figurative details. Both buildings are effectively billboards for their respective companies, each proudly bearing the name of Polívka's client.

86Ah   Obecní Dům (Municipal House) 1905–12

Námestí Republicky 5/1090, Staré Město

Antonín Balšánek and Osvald Polívka

M námestí Republicky

This is one of the most opulent and well-known buildings of this period, with accessible interiors, comprising a concert hall, as well as a café, restaurant and beer-hall. The interior plan of the building is quite complex, so as to accommodate so many functions on a difficult site. The larger spaces of the concert hall, entrance and restaurant rooms are balanced by single-height corridors of smaller rooms on the first floor. These corridors run parallel to the balconies in the restaurant rooms. Despite its renown as a key example of Art Nouveau, the Municipal House demonstrates an eclectic approach to decoration rather than a concern for unity of style. Balšánek

and Polívka's design reveals the still-strong influence of the Baroque revival of the 1870s and 1880s within Czech Art Nouveau, and the influence of Parisian models, such as the Opera and the Grand Palais.

The architects enlisted the services of leading Czech artists, including Ladislav Šaloun and Josef Maratka, who were responsible for the main façade decoration (with mosaic designs by Karel Spillar). The interior salons and concert hall were decorated with paintings by Jan Preisler, Alfons Mucha and Max Švabinský. Mucha's paintings explore the Folk themes of his famous *Slav Epic*.

87AI **Vinohrady Theatre** 1905–9
náměstí Míru 2/1450, Vinohrady
Alois Čenský

M náměstí Míru

This theatre is a dramatic and curious mix of Art Nouveau decoration with more traditional figural sculpture based on historicist and mythic themes. Čenský had won the competition to design the theatre in 1903, with a building concieved in a Neo-Renaissance style. Once work began, more modern features were added to the decoration by sculptor Bohumil Kafka. The two winged figure groups representing *Opera* and *Drama*, which crown the building, are by Milan Havlícek. The decoration inside the building is also impressive.

88Bb **Villa Sucharda** 1906–7
Slavíčkova 6/24, Bubeneč
Jan Kotěra

M Hradčanská

Like the examples by Jan Koula and Dušan Jurkovič on the adjacent plots **71, 89**, Folk architecture provided the inspiration for this villa and studio, designed for the sculptor Stanislav Sucharda. As well as the local vernacular, first put to use by Kotěra in the design of the Trmal villa, Strašnice (1902), he also makes great use of the 'English style' of domestic planning. English architectural attitudes (published widely abroad) helped Czech architects in their search for a greater freedom of plan to meet modern needs. The living rooms of the house are planned around their garden aspect, with the kitchen and service rooms on the street side. The studio wing, which has a small turreted spiral staircase, is connected to the main house by a single storey, which contains the library.

The path to nationhood

89Bb **Villa Náhlovský** 1907

Suchardova 4/284, Bubeneč

Dušan Jurkovič

M Hradčanská

Next to Kotěra, the Slovak Dušan Jurkovič (1868–1947) was the major exponent of Folk architecture in the Czech lands in the early years of the twentieth century, but this is the only example of his work in Prague. Whereas Kotěra reigned supreme in Prague, Jurkovič's influence extended further east, in Slovakia and Hungary, where the Folk revival had been in full swing for a decade or more. His best-known work is the Luhačovice Spa in Moravia. He also worked on numerous projects that were Folk-oriented, including buildings for the 1895 Ethnographic Exhibition in Prague. This villa is typical of his work, inspired by both Slavic wooden architecture and Scandinavian vernacular. Like others, Jurkovič's preoccupations directed him towards Modernism later in his career.

90AI **Lucerna Palace** 1907–21

Vodičkova 36/704, Nové Město

Václav Havel

M Müstek

The Lucerna is most remarkable for being the first reinforced concrete building in Prague. Occupying the site between Vodičkova and Štěpánská, it contains a passageway with shops, restaurants, a cinema and large concert hall. The building was built in two sections: the Vodičkova wing was built between 1907 and 1913; the Štěpánská wing was begun in 1913 and completed after the war. This type of arcaded building, housing entertainment and commercial facilities, became a standard model in Prague. Havel, the grandfather of the dissident playwright and later president, Václav Havel, was a successful developer, who worked on this project with the engineer Stanislav Bechyně. Since returning to the private ownership of the Havel family in 1989 there has been some dispute over the future of the building, and the possible redevelopment of the site.

91Bf **Villa Kotěra** 1908–9

Hradešínská 6/1542, Vinohrady

Jan Kotěra

M 16, 22

By 1908, Kotěra's ideal of the functional family villa was almost fully resolved. His own house in Vinohrady shows how, by this point, he had managed to discard all unnecessary ornamentation, concentrating instead upon a language of constructional elements and the poetry of materials. The unrendered brick surfaces and flat roofs show the influence of Frank Lloyd Wright. The plan of the house was to become a standard for modern villas – a central hall, the living areas facing the garden, connected to the outside by a series of terraces. The street side of the house is austere and functional, with small windows denoting the interior arrangement. Kotěra is buried in the nearby Vinohrady cemetery.

92Bf **Laichter House** 1908–9

Chopinova 4/1543, Vinohrady

Jan Kotěra

M Jířího z Poděbrad; T 11

Kotěra's building for the radical publisher, Jan Laichter, combined office space for his publishing house with living accommodation. The brick façade has a central protruding section forming a balcony above. The organisation of the façade describes the different functions of each floor. The only ornamentation is provided by the patterning of the brickwork; a more restrained example of the kind of brick Modernism pioneered in Europe by Hendrik Berlage and Peter Behrens. The structural emphasis of Kotěra's design was a progressive step compared to the still popular Art Nouveau buildings of other architects.

The path to nationhood

93Ag Štenc House 1909–10
Salvátorská 8/931, Staré Město
Otakar Novotný

M Staroměstská

The commissioning of progressive buildings by avant-garde publishers gave young architects the chance to break away from the more traditional expectations of other clients. Novotný was one of Kotěra's pupils, hence the similarity to Kotěra's brick buildings of the same time. The flat brick front and courtyard façades are almost totally unornamented, the entrance is concealed to one side of a glazed white brick colonnade on the street side. The attic studio has a glazed front wall, curving over to allow maximum light. Inside, the double-height graphic design studio is open plan, divided by a gallery with a spiral iron staircase. This studio looks out onto the courtyard through a large rectangular window, running the length of the room. The spatial purity of the building provided a blueprint for later Functionalist projects.

94Ad Hlávka Bridge 1909–11
Nové Město
Pavel Janák

M Vltavská; T 3, 8

This is a very early work by Janák, before his development of a Cubist language, which shows his ability to enliven construction with the simplest of formal devices. This bridge replaced an earlier one, and was built in two sections, each of a different style and material. The southern part was in steel. The northern concrete section, spanning the section of the bridge across Štvanice island, was designed by Janák, and has the effect of a single undulating line following the rise and fall of the arches underneath. The inset statues above each pier on Janák's side are by Štursa and date from 1911–13. The bridge was widened in the late 1950s, when the steel section was replaced with a concrete section. The form of Janák's design was continued to give the bridge uniformity.

95Ab **Villa Bílek** 1910–11
Mickiewiczova 1/233, Hradčany
František Bílek

M Hradčanská

František Bílek was a Symbolist artist who designed and built this studio house for himself and his family. Modern allegorical Symbolism did not find an architectural application quite like this anywhere else in Prague. The villa is an extension of Bílek's sculptural work, in which he combined a strong belief in nature with a set of more mystical *fin-de-siècle* concerns. As a student, first in Prague and then in Paris, Bílek had developed a strong spiritual and moral artistic direction, influenced by both his religious upbringing and his interest in medieval art. He turned from painting to sculpture, and worked across a range of media in the applied and graphic arts. His interests set him apart from his Viennese-influenced contemporaries in Prague at the beginning of the twentieth century. His house, which seems isolated despite its close proximity to other residences, seems to bear witness to this peculiar place in Czech modern art. The villa, a plain geometric brick building, is dominated by the columns that form a curved colonnade around most of the façade. The columns were designed by Bílek to look like bundles of wheat – a symbol of natural sustenance. The villa is now a museum to Bílek. It retains its original interiors, including some of his rough-hewn furniture, as well as a collection of his paintings, sculpture and ceramics.

96Bf **Municipal House** 1910–11
Hybešova 10/14, Karlín
Josef Sakař

M Křížíkova; T 8, 22

The organisation of Prague's new suburbs had been partly determined by the establishment of the district of Karlín after 1817 **48**. These suburbs were given the right to their own administrations, and some, like Karlín, were granted the status of 'royal town' in 1904. Each district had its own 'National' House, to provide for municipal and cultural functions. This building is a particularly fine example, and should be compared to the Municipal House **86** in the centre of Prague. It is an Art Nouveau building with Neo-classical decoration, set in large gardens. It now belongs to the Czech Radio Company, and has been considerably altered; the original cafés, restaurant and theatre are no longer there. The rest of Karlín is an elegant, if rather shabby, residential area, with Neo-Baroque and Art Nouveau apartment buildings.

On the same street is an **apartment building** (Hybešova 5/519) built in the same year and designed by Emil Králíček with Matěj Blecha.

The path to nationhood

97Ak **Urbánek House (Mozarteum)** 1911–12
Jungmannova 30/745, Nové Město
Jan Kotěra

M Narodní třída

The music publisher, Mojmir Urbánek, commissioned Kotěra to design this building, which combines commercial premises with a family apartment and a concert hall. The brick façade is contained within a large exposed reinforced concrete frame. As with the Laichter House of 1908 **92**, Kotěra has made clear in the design of the façade the difference between the residential and commercial functions. Above the first storey, the façade gradually recedes within its frame, as if it were layered, rather like a stack of playing cards. The entrance is marked by two figurative sculptures by Jan Štursa, above which is a continuous band of windows on the office floor. The living accommodation is arranged on the uppermost floors. The severe brick gable gives the building a monumentality that sets it apart from the other buildings of the street. Overall, it was one of the most uncompromising buildings of the pre-war generation, and displays a rationalism and austerity that makes it a landmark in the development of Czech Modernism.

98Ag **Adam Pharmacy** 1911–13
Václavské náměstí 8/775, Nové Město
Emil Králíček and Matěj Blecha

M Müstek

This small *lekarna* (pharmacy) is easy to miss when Wenceslas Square is crowded. Králíček trained under Joseph Maria Olbrich at the Darmstadt Applied Arts School, and Olbrich's influence is apparent in the narrow façade. Králíček and Blecha also worked together on Cubist projects such as the Díamant House **108**. Although the Adam Pharmacy is not strictly a Cubist building, it is possible to see the connection here between late Secessionist and early Cubist geometric details.

99AI Koruna Palace 1912–14

Václavské náměstí 1/846, Nové Město

Antonín Pfeiffer

M Müstek

The preference for a more geometric form of ornamentation, which replaced the naturalistic decoration of earlier Art Nouveau buildings, is shown in
several buildings on Wenceslas Square. Pfeiffer had
been a pupil of Kotěra, and, like many, practised a
form of Modernism, but with a marked tendency
towards the decorative. It is also possible to detect
the influence of Josef Hoffmann's Palais Stoclet.
Like the Šupich Building 100 across the road, Pfeiffer's
Koruna Palace has a corner tower topped with a
crown shaped turret. The use of decoration is
simpler, with broad expanses of glass filling the
frame of the lower three storeys. The building is
multi-functional – a passage for shops connects the
neighbouring streets, and there was even a swimming pool in the basement. The building has recently undergone massive restoration – it appears
to have been entirely stripped and reconstructed
inside – and has become a popular commercial let
due to its prime site.

100AI Šupich Building 1913–16

Václavské náměstí 38/795, Nové Město

Matěj Blecha and Petr Kropáček

M Müstek

Adjacent to the Lucerna Palace **90**, this corner
building forms part of the redevelopment of this
large commercial site on the corner of Wenceslas
Square. The building represents a rather different
approach to the Modern style – a kind of 'machine
aesthetic', which uses mechanisistic motifs as a
form of ornamentation. The overall effect of the
building is rather like a giant piston engine, reminiscent of something from the set of Fritz Lang's film
Metropolis, or Sant'Elia's sketchbooks. Exotic
egyptian heads mark the division between each
vertical section. The roof is covered in copper and
has a series of attic windows lighting the top storey
studio rooms. The building attracted some criticism
from advocates of a purist and unornamented
architecture. It was described by Otakar Novotný as
an 'architectural monster'.

The path to nationhood

101 Ab   **Residential Complex** 1912–14
Na valech 24–28, Hradčany
František Velich and Jan Žák

M Hradčanská

The issue of worker and public housing was one of central concern to architects in the interwar period. Experimental garden suburbs, popular with the middle classes in the early 1920s, later gave way to social housing projects. Before World War I, the standard tenement block was the narrow triple-bay block, often very dark with inadequate sanitation. Technical improvements in construction, ventilation and the provision of water to tall blocks had already made some impact by 1914. This small, experimental complex, arranged around a large courtyard, anticipated the later emphasis on 'healthy housing'. Instead of being cramped and narrow, only two bays were used, giving each apartment a wider aspect on to both the street and the gardens behind.

102 Ao   **Hlava Institute of Pathology** 1913–21
Studničkova 2–4/2039, Nové Město
Alois Špalek

M Karlovo náměstí; T 18, 24

Set in the university district, the Institute of Pathology appears at first to be a standard administrative building. However, the rear side of the building shows how Viennese-trained Špalek has created a building that adeptly serves its function. The demand for well-lit laboratory space resulted in this sweep of semi-circular glazed bay windows and the wider ribbon windows of the autopsy rooms. All the windows have metal frames, so that the laboratory side of the building looks like a series of interlocking glasshouses, now, unfortunately, in a bad state of disrepair.

Czech Cubism 1910–25

03Ag Lamppost 1912

Jungmannovo náměstí, Nové Město

Emil Králíček and Matěj Blecha

M Müstek

This is a stone, carved lamppost with a seat at the base. It was erected in 1912 and designed (it is now thought) by Králíček at the time he was working with Blecha's construction company, in particular on the Díamant department store **108**. The lamppost is a simple repetition of Cubist forms, also reminiscent of Romanian sculptor Constantin Brancusi's *Endless Column*. The Díamant building demonstrates the same heavily scored Cubistic forms as the lamppost and, together with the Adam Pharmacy **98**, show how Králíček deftly incorporated Cubism into his Secessionist way of working, treating it as an extension of his geometric decorative vocabulary.

04Ah House at the Black Madonna 1911–12

Celetná 34/569, Staré Mesto

Josef Gočár

M náměstí Republicky

Gočár's famous commercial building is one of the best known examples of Cubism in Prague. It was commissioned in 1911 by businessman František Herbst as a department store, which would replace Herbst's previous premises on this site. Gočár used a reinforced concrete frame for the building, which allowed him to be more creative with the interior space on such an awkward site, and to create wide, deep-set window openings. The weightiness of the mansard roof is broken up with angular dormer windows.

Originally, the first floor of the building was a café. Period photographs show a heavy wooden interior with dramatic metal light fittings. In 1993–94, the

building was reconstructed by Karel Prager, and is now in use as the permanent gallery of Czech Cubist art and design from the National Gallery, the Museum of Decorative Arts and the National Technical Museum. Plans were made to restore Gočár's first-floor café, but as nothing remained of that interior, the reconstruction was not carried out. Prager's design preserved what original details there were

93

Czech Cubism

(such as the dramatic metal staircase) as well as removing partition walls to show Gočár's original structure. Prager also opened out the building at the top with a glass roof extension above the stairwell. There are now two exhibition floors of Cubist art and design, as well as a further two floors of temporary

exhibition space. The ground-floor façade has been renewed in the style of a shop exterior of the period, and this floor now houses a bookshop. On the corner of the building is preserved a small Madonna statue from the original seventeenth-century structure, which gives the building its name.

105Ao Villa Kovařovič 1911–12

Libušina 3/49, Vyšehrad

Josef Chochol

T 3, 7, 17

Chochol's substantial family villa occupies a prime site overlooking the Vltava below Vyšehrad, although it is now isolated by a busy traffic junction. Here Chochol achieves a particularly pure application of Cubist forms, most noticeably on the side walls of the house, where the play of light across the facets gives the effect of folded paper – or perhaps the diamond vaulted interior of a Gothic chapel. The Cubist style is applied to the layout of the paths and gardens as far as the boundary wall, as well as to

details like the ironwork and window frames. Sadly, Chochol's original interiors were removed some time ago.

106Ao Triple house complex 1912–13

Rašínovo nábřeží 6/42, 8/47, 10/71, Vyšehrad

Josef Chochol

T 3, 7, 17

This comprises a complex of three self-contained villas, built for clients Jan and Josef Bayer, Antonín Belada and František Hodek. Like the nearby Villa Kovařovič **105**, the houses were both designed for and built by prominent construction firms (in this

case, Belada and Hodek). The middle house has a central gabled entrance with sculpted decoration in the gable. The other two houses have their entrances to each side of the complex. There is a lack of continuity between the three elements of the design, which may well have been intentional, but gives the building a rather confused appearance, as if it were a random jumble of Cubistic elements, its concept never fully resolved. With its mansard roof and long, low appearance, the building looks rather like a side wing or stable block of a Baroque palace.

07Ao   **Hodek Apartment Building** 1913–14

Neklanova 30/98, Vyšehrad

Josef Chochol

T 3, 7, 17

This apartment complex, built by František Hodek (one of Chochol's main clients and construction firms), demonstrates all the key principles of Cubist design. The repetition of diamond forms on the façade echoes the site plan. The building is oriented to the corner junction, so that the façade appears to push outwards and upwards – a much more dynamic composition than Chochol's nearby villas, which retain a classical plan. The Hodek apartment block goes further than other Cubist projects. The windows are distorted in the same manner as the rest of the façade, for instance. If the light is right, and you stand in the right place, you can get the full effect of the optical illusion that is Cubism. However, as with all Cubist buildings it is still essentially a cosmetic exercise – the interior is Cubist in its detail and decoration rather than its plan, and the rear façade of the building bears little resemblance to the two main street façades. Chochol's design method was, apparently, to mark out a grid pattern on an elevation plan, pinpointing where the diagonal lines could converge and cross to create the most dynamic effect. On this particular building, his method appears clearest.

Further down Neklanova Street, at no. 2, is a building of 1912–13, which echoes, with less severity, the Hodek block. It was built by developer Antonín Belada, and it is possible that Chochol was also involved in the design.

108Ak   **Díamant House** 1912–13

Spálená 4/82, Nové Město

Emil Králíček

M Národní třída

This commercial and residential building was one of several projects designed by Králíček for the building firm of Matěj Blecha between 1903–13. Králíček is one of the 'forgotten' Cubists. His works have often previously been attributed to Blecha, who he worked closely with. He had trained with Josef Maria Olbrich in Darmstadt, and the Díamant Building represents his shift from Art Nouveau to a more recognisable Cubist language. It has interesting Cubistic ironwork both inside and out, including the staircase railings, and light fittings. Between the building and the Baroque Church of the Holy Trinity (1712–13) is Králíček's famous Cubist archway, designed in 1912 to frame the 1717 statue of St John of Nepomuk. This was much discussed at the time, as obvious parallels can be drawn between the Baroque and Cubism, although much of the criticism was negative. More recently, the building was converted to house a car showroom, the ground floor windows replaced by a larger glazed wall.

Czech Cubism

109Bc Cemetery Entrance Gate and Kiosks 1912–14
Ďáblická, Ďáblice
Vlastislav Hofman

B 103, 258

Although Hofman was employed by the municipal building department, he is not known for many architectural projects, and this is possibly his only realised design. His work in the applied arts was considerably more significant, particularly his designs for the cooperative workshop, Artěl. The Cemetery gates were built by the municipality to Hofman's design – a simple curved colonnade with entrance kiosks at either end. In addition to this arrangement, Hofman designed an imposing mortuary, but this was not built.

110Ab Two-Family House 1912–13
Tychonova 4/268, 6/269, Hradčany
Josef Gočár

M Hradčanská

These two semi-detached villas were designed for Karel Hofmann and Jan Stach of the Municipal Insurance Company. Gočár's design was essentially rather traditional – a classical villa design with projecting mansard roof, like the House at the Black Madonna 104. The restrained Cubist elements, largely confined to the entrance bay and doorway, were added to the design before construction was underway.

111Ac Teachers' Housing Cooperative Building 1917–19
Elisky Krásnohorské 10–14/123, 1021, 1037, Staré Město
Otakar Novotný

M Staroměstská

This was the first of Novotný's projects for the Teachers' Housing Cooperative; it was followed by a 1923 project 116. It is a three-section block containing three to four room apartments. Novotný's use of applied colour (reds and yellows, now much faded) is not so common in early Cubist buildings and indicates the more flamboyant decorative style of Rondo Cubism, which took hold in the 1920s. Novotný's utilitarian organisation of the building owes more to the influence of his tutor, Jan Kotěra, than it does to the formalist preoccupations of the Cubists prior to World War I.

12Ag Commercial Building 1920–22
Jungmannovo náměstí, 4/764 & 28 Října 8,
Nové Město

Rudolf Stockar

M Můstek

This narrow building, hardly noticeable now on the crowded street, was the first to show the development Cubism took after World War I. The two façades of the building are rather different from one another. On 28 Října the façade is plainer and more geometrical, whereas the façade on Jungmannova is fully-fledged Rondo Cubism, comprising rounded forms with the use of colour (red and white like the Czech flag). Stockar was the director of the applied arts collective, Artěl, and contributed to the new Folkloric tendency in Cubism with his interior and furniture design in the 1920s.

113Bb Wooden Cottages 1921–22
Prague Zoological Gardens, U trojského zámek, Troja

Josef Gočár

M Nádraži Holešovice; B 112

These two timber cottages were first built at Kbely airport, and later moved to their current position in the grounds of the Zoo. In order to find them, you must pay to enter the Zoo and walk through as far as you can go, past the Lion House to the scrubland at the back. They are worth a visit, as they are among the few examples of Rondo-Cubist Folk architecture ever built. Gočár has tried to fuse modern Cubist elements onto a traditional architecture, using the colours of the Czech national flag to add a further dimension to this National Style. Unfortunately, during the buildings' move to their present site, preservation work was undertaken that protected the wood from decay, but removed all the painted colour.

Czech Cubism

114Ah **Czechoslovak Legiobank** 1921–23

Na poříčí 24/1046, Nové Město

Josef Gočár

M náměstí Republicky

Designed for a competition, Gočár's first major commercial commission after World War I is perhaps the best example of the struggle to create a National Style derived from Cubism and Czech vernacular. The bank commemorates the Czech Legion, national heroes of the war. The façade is inscribed with 'Unity', the slogan of the Legion's competition. The sculptural reliefs on the lower portion of the façade, by Jan Štursa and Otto Gutfreund, depict images from the war and relate to the unification of the Czechoslovak states. Above the first storey, the regular cylindrical treatment of the façade derives from Rondo Cubism. Originally the façade was red and white, but the colours are now faded and hardly visible. The interiors have recently been restored, and there the colours have been renewed to their original vibrancy. The red and white painted metal grilles used on the staircase, for example, were designed in collaboration with František Kysela. Like Janák's Adria Palace **115**, designed a year later, Gočár's building shows a shift away from the jagged geometry of the earlier Cubist buildings, towards a monumental symmetry that is closer to

Renaissance models. The dynamism of earlier Cubist buildings is replaced by a stress on decoration and sculptural detail. The interior of the main hall of the bank is lavishly decorated with the same Rondo-Cubistic forms, in both mosaic and marble, and lit by an elegant glass-domed roof in the main hall. It is very likely that this interior was a direct reference to Otto Wagner's 1904 Vienna Postal Savings Bank.

115Ag **Adria Palace** 1922–25

Jungmannova 31/36, Nové Město

Pavel Janák, with Joseph Zasche

M Můstek

Built for the Riunione Adriatica di Sicurta insurance offices, the building now houses a film club and, in the basement, the experimental Laterna Magika Theatre. Designed in the style of a Venetian Renaissance palace, the façade treatment shows the later decorative tendencies of Rondo Cubism. Despite its obvious references, the palace was not simply a return to historicist monumental architecture, but a bizarre attempt to combine a modern decorative language with traditional and symbolic forms, sometimes (and misleadingly) referred to as Czech 'Art Deco'. The building attracted Le Corbusier's scorn when he visited Prague in 1925. Almost as soon as it was completed, Janák had rejected his attempts at creating a National Style, and instead turned to a more Functionalist way of building. The Adria is one of the most extraordinary modern buildings in this part of Prague, not least because it is the result of such a complex and conflicting ideology. In 1997,

it was undergoing renovation, and exterior cleaning was beginning to reveal even more extraordinary detail than was previously visible.

The group of bronze figures on the Národní façade is by Jan Štursa. Other sculptural decoration is by Otto Gutfreund, K. Dvořák and B. Kafka. The building's arcade and upstairs interiors are richly decorated. The staircase leading from the arcade towards the terrace restaurant is decorated with motifs relating to film and theatre. During the 1989 revolution, the building was used briefly as the headquarters of Civic Forum.

16Bb Teachers' Cooperative Apartment Building
1923

Kamenická 35/811, Holešovice

Otakar Novotný

M Vltavská; T 1, 8, 25, 26

Of Novotný's two residential complexes 111 for the Teachers' Housing Cooperative, the second in Holešovice demonstrates his experimentation with Rondo Cubist forms. The bulging convex sections between each window are a departure from the 'folded' prismatic sections in pre-war Cubist buildings. On a terraced façade they create an arresting, if rather heavy and ugly, interplay. However, Novotný was to become increasingly disillusioned with Cubism, and his later projects looked further afield to Modernist developments and away from the essential decorativism of these buildings.

◄17Ah Anglo-Czechoslovak Bank 1923–25

Hybernská 5/1034, Nové Město

Josef Gočár

M náměstí Republicky

Not to be confused with the Czech Legiobank nearby 114, Gočár's addition to the Sweerts-Sporck Palace fits in well with the Baroque character of the older palace (designed by Anton Haffenecker in 1783), in a manner which confirms the relationship between Cubism and the Baroque. Behind the original façade, Gočár added an annex, with an extended gable characteristic of his work at Hradec Králové in the same years. The added storeys mirror the articulation of Haffenecker's façade, but hardly interfere with the original building.

National Monument 131

Between the wars:
the new Czechoslovak state 1918–38

18Bb Dejvice New Plan 1920–24
Vitežné náměstí, Dejvice
Antonín Engel

M Dejvická

The establishment of the State Planning Commission in 1920, followed by the Greater Prague Act of 1921, was recognition of the need for a coherent programme of urban planning for the city. The programme covered the reform of residential, transportation, economic and sanitary needs. Key areas of the city were designated for special development. Although several of these projects were never carried out, Engel's plan for Dejvice met with state approval. He proposed a town planning system based on the theories of Otto Wagner – a monumental architecture, planned around wide boulevards, which fanned out from central circular intersec-

tions. The centre of the Dejvice plan is Vitežné náměstí (Victory Square). Engel's project met with disapproval in the the pages of avant-garde journals, where it was criticised for being outdated. The surrounding area of Dejvice is particularly interesting for its interwar architecture, especially its schools, housing and university buildings.

19Be Ořechovka Garden Suburb 1919–25
Macharovo náměstí, Střešovice
Jaroslav Vondrák and Jan Šenkýř

M Dejvická; T 1, 2, 18

Jan Kotěra had pioneered the introduction of English Garden City principles before World War I. He experimented with these at two other Czech towns: the new town of Hradec Králové and the railway workers' colony at Louny. Vondrák, Kotěra's pupil, and Šenkýř won a competition organised in 1919 by the Building Cooperative of Public Servants, to plan the district of Ořechovka. A grid plan of streets surrounds the central garden square (Macharovo náměstí). Vondrák was heavily influenced by the theories of Ebenezer Howard and Raymond Unwin (who visited Prague to lecture in 1922), consequently the district has the character of an English suburb. There are twenty-nine different variants of house type in the quarter, mostly semi-detached. To one side of the central square is a community

Between the wars

building, containing shops, a restaurant and now a cinema. As well as the standard houses, there are a number of bespoke villas. The most interesting of these are the four studio-villas designed by Pavel Janák in 1923–24 for some of Prague's leading artists. These villas are built of exposed brick work, with Dutch-style steep pantile roofs. These are: **Cukrovarnická 24** designed for the painter Vincenc Beneš; **Na Ořechovce 41** for Bohumil Kafka; and the pair of houses at **Lomená 10** and 12 the former for the painter Emil Filla. Vondrák's own family house, built in 1923, is at **Žapadni 21**, which has a large curved frontage, with a stepped roofline and central chimney.

Žapadni 21

120Af **Prague Castle renovation** 1920 onwards
Praszký hrad, Hradčany
Josip Plečnik and Otto Rothmayer
Ⓜ Hradčanská

Slovenian-born architect Plečnik (1871–1957) was first invited to Prague by his friend, Jan Kotěra, in 1910, taking over as Professor of the School of Arts and Crafts in 1911. In 1920, he won the competition to redesign the castle gardens and was consequently invited by President Masaryk to become the castle architect. The first stage of redevelopment was the redesign of the presidential apartments in the South wing, followed by his new layouts for the first and third courtyards. Plečnik's appointment aroused a great deal of controversy and bitter argument, partly on nationalist grounds. He was accused of introducing foreign elements into the castle and destroying its homogeneity. In fact, his additions echoed the Neo-classical architecture of the eighteenth-century castle, as well as emphasising the eclectic character of the castle's development. Plečnik's decorative work is reminiscent of Egyptian, Assyrian and Slavonic forms, as well those of antiquity. After the mid-1920s, Plečnik's visits to Prague became less frequent. He stayed in Ljubljana and conducted his supervision of the project largely through correspondence. Also at this time, he discussed with Masaryk the urban redevelopment of the area surrounding the castle, a project that came to nothing. Despite Pavel Janák's appointment as castle architect in 1936, Plečnik's work continued, supervised by his student and disciple, Otto Rothmayer. Plečnik's use of Neo-classical details as both structure and ornament – the placing of

Bull staircase

Garden terrace

Garden obelisk

Rothmayer's staircase

obelisks, pergolas and columns – as well as his use of sumptuous materials creates an unusual relationship of periods and styles that we might now call Postmodernism.

Plečnik's distinctive imprint can be seen in the three main inner gardens of the Castle: Rajská (1920–25), Na Valech (1920–25), and Na baště (1920–24). From the third courtyard, the Rajská, or paradise garden, is reached via the Bull Staircase, a sculpted metal and stone staircase ornamented with bulls' heads, which leads into the garden via a Neo-classical stairwell. In the garden there is an observation terrace and several other architectural details, such as obelisks by Plečnik. In the third

courtyard, there is a monolith by Plečnik, erected to commemorate the first decade of the Republic in 1928. Plečnik's interiors for the presidential apartments (occasionally open to the public) are decorated with marble, inlaid wood, and Neo-classical furniture. The apartments are in the South wing. Just off from the Matthias Gateway, at the entrance to the second courtyard, is the Hall of Columns, with Otto Rothmayer's spiral staircase. Rothmayer continued Plečnik's reconstruction work on the eighteenth-century sections of the Castle after the latter left Prague.

Plečnik's contribution to the castle underwent extensive restoration during 1992–94, and was the subject of a major exhibition held at the castle in 1994.

121Bh Podolí Municipal Waterworks 1923–28

Podolská 17/15, Podolí

Antonín Engel

T 3, 17, 64

Engel's water filtration works building was designed in a heavy and monumental Neo-classical style, which consists of a rather monotonous repetition of basic, 'stripped' Classical elements. Engel, in his capacity as professor at the Technical University, combined rationalist teachings with a belief in the eternal qualities of monumental Classicism. This kind of stolid, municipally-approved style is very different to the witty and inventive form of Classi-

cism which was being used by Plečnik at the same time. Since its recent repainting, the building looks less dour, and the whitewash has brought a kind of jazzy, Art Deco feel to it, as well as highlighted some of the decorative detail.

Between the wars

122Bf Rural Education Building 1924–26
Slezská 7/100, Vinohrady
Josef Gočár

M náměstí Miru

Gočár's monumentalist projects from the mid 1920s show his concern for combining a Classical composition with a modern, unadorned appearence. This huge, rather unforgiving administrative building on a jut of land between Vinohradska and Slezská streets has an interesting plan: a central section flanked by two taller elements, which hints at the kind of pyramidal composition he used on several buildings, including the secondary school in Hradec

Králové, built in the same year. The façade of the building on Slezská is of exposed brickwork.

123Ak Škoda Building 1925
Jungmannova 29/35, Nové Mesto
Pavel Janák

M Můstek

The Adria Palace 115, begun the preceding year, was to be Janák's last Rondo-Cubist project; the adjacent Škoda Building shows a kind of return to order. Unlike the variety of forms found on the Adria, Janák used a system of repeated rectangles on the Škoda Building, which gradually increase in thickness the higher up the façade they go, casting deep shadows. The building is topped with a heavy cornice, and a recessed top storey. Like Gočár's

commercial and industrial projects of the mid 1920s, this is a very grim architecture, despite showing the ways in which both architects were attempting to develop a geometric Modernism.

124Ak Olympic Department Store 1925–28
Spálená 16/75, Nové Mĕsto
Jaromír Krejcar

M Národni třida

Krejcar was already advocating the 'technical marvel' of skyscrapers as a student in 1921, and this idea was reinforced by the publication of Le Corbusier's city theories of the early 1920s. Perhaps the most important theorist of technical architecture at the time, Krejcar was a member both of Devĕstil and the Czech wing of CIAM (Congrès Internationaux d'Architecture Moderne). Designs for the Olympic building were first produced in 1923, but construction did not begin until 1925. It was envisaged as a Devĕstil manifesto – an architectural collage for modern life – a glass-walled envelope, replete with the ephemeral signifiers of metropolitan living, including advertising signs, new typography, neon lights, striped awnings and a cinema. The steel railings evoked another emblem of modernity – the ocean liner. However, the final result does not do justice to Krejcar's initial vision

(the façade is too solid to be thought of as a glass skin), although it is still one of the most important and earliest Functionalist projects in the city.

The upper floors contain offices and apartments, the lower three floors are occupied by shops and restaurant facilities. Above the glass, arcaded entrance, the shop floors are fronted by continuous bands of fenestration. The interior, although shabby and crowded with temporary partitions, still retains its character, particularly in what can still be seen of the central atrium.

125 Bf **Apartment Buildings** 1925–26

Bulharská 29–41/714–20, 705–711, Vršovice

František Libra

B 135

Between Ruská and Bulharská streets, Libra built these flats for low-income families using the system of open-corridor planning. In order to save space, the access corridors are on the outside of the building. This type of plan, utilised in various modified forms by architects like Libra and Rudolf Hrabě, were promoted as healthy and economical forms of functional housing in the later 1920s, during the first stage of modern, high-density housing development in the city.

126 Bi **Spořilov Garden Suburb** 1925–29

Spořilov

Planned by Josef Bertl and Josef Barek

B 170, 178, 203

The speculative dwellings of the garden quarter of Spořilov are of a rather different character to the 'bespoke' villas of Ořechovka and Baba. Financed by the Savings Bank of Vinohrady, the quarter consists of about 1,000 two or three-storey houses, mostly semi-detached or detached. There are also some small terraces of worker housing, all set amidst allotment gardens. There are nine different dwelling types. The informal planning and 'cottage' character of some of the housing shows the influence of the English Garden City. However, the mix is eclectic: some of the other houses have flat roofs and sun terraces with tubular steel railings, all of them designed by Karel Polívka and Vlastimil Brožek.

The quarter is planned around a long, sloping central square, Roztylské náměstí, which has an elegant modern church on the higher slopes of the square. The quarter was also supplied with restaurants and shops. Much of the housing was built from prefabricated elements and concrete blocks manufactured on site.

Between the wars

127 Bb **Veletržní (Trade Fairs) Palace** 1924–28
Dukelských hrdinu no. 45/530, Holešovice
Oldřich Tyl and Josef Fuchs

T 5, 12, 17

In 1924, a competition was organised to design an exhibition building to house the Prague Sample and Trade Fairs in the Holešovice district, close to the exhibition park. The final commission was awarded to Oldřich Tyl, along with Josef Fuchs, whose interior plans were thought to best suit the function of the building. The architects developed what can best be described as an exemplar of Scientific Functionalism, which was the earliest of its kind in Europe. On a visit to Prague in 1930, Le Corbusier famously commented that, having seen the Trade Fair Building, he 'understood how to create large constructions'.

The final plan was prepared betweeen 1924 and 1928. The building has eight storeys and is of reinforced concrete construction. The exterior is entirely plain, and the continuous window strips give the impression of a completely glass walled building. It is planned around a central atrium, with a ground floor exhibition space and surrounding galleries leading from corridors on all the above floors. The building also has two basement floors, containing a cinema, and on the eighth floor there is a restaurant with a roof terrace.

In the postwar period the building lost its function as the site for major trade fairs. It was almost completely destroyed by fire in 1974. In 1978, it was designated as the future National Gallery of Modern Art, but did not open as such until 1995. The reconstruction work was led by Miroslav Masák and the SIAL team **175**. The new Centre for Modern and Contemporary Art contains three floors of modern European art from the National Galleries Collections, as well as a number of exhibition spaces for temporary shows, a restaurant and a good bookstore. The reconstruction work has been faithful to the original design, so that the Tyl and Fuchs design can be understood, and the integrity of the building is preserved.

128 Bc **Electricity Company Palace** 1926–31
Bubenská 1/1477, Holešovice
Adolf Benš and Josef Kříž

M Vltavská

Near to the Hlávka Bridge is the building that is now the headquarters of the Prague Transport Company, which also houses the Holešovice Community Health centre. It was the result of a limited competition to design the administrative centre of the Electricity Company. The architects' winning design featured a corridor access plan that was influential on the subsequent planning of public buildings. In order to realise their plan, the architects were allowed to alter the development plan of this area of the city. The central eight-storey block has a full height top lit entrance hall. The central core is flanked by two six-storey wings, to which a wide three-storey entrance wing was added on each side. The interior, which is accessible to general visitors only as far as the entrance hall, still shows all the original detailing, now in need of repair and renova- tion. The exterior of the building is clad in white ceramic tiles. In the basement of the building is a galleried lecture hall, as well as public bath facilites. Like Tyl and Fuchs' Veletržní Palace 127, this building demonstrates the mature application of Functionalist principles to large-scale projects by architects early in their careers, and the willingness of the state to support such projects.

129Ba Villa Linhart 1927–29

Na viničných horách 46, Hanspaulka

Evžen Linhart

M Dejvická; B131

This is a large Modernist villa on a corner plot in the garden district of Hanspaulka, designed by the architect for his own family. The design demonstrates all the quintessential elements of Modernist planning, borrowing from Adolf Loos' 'Raumplan' concept and Le Corbusier's domestic designs, and is one of the earliest of its type in Prague. The building is a complex assembly of geometric volumes – the concrete frame of the pergola on first-floor level is an echo of the interior. Inside, the living areas are linked by ramps to create a series of interpenetrating spaces. The house is now in a rather fragile state, the rendering coming away from the building in large chunks, but still looks remarkable amidst its mature garden. In the same road, there is a contemporaneous house by Linhart's colleague Jan Rosůlek (Na viničných horách 44), also built for the architect's family. This villa was substantially altered by Vladimír Grégr in the late 1930s.

130Ag Municipal Library 1924–28

Mariánské náměstí 98, Nové Město

František Roith

M Staroměstská

This is an attempt to provide a simplified modern version of the Baroque city palaces of the Old Town, which would be suitable for civic buildings, but would not disturb the historic character of the surroundings. This 'palace type' had been devised for a number of ministerial buildings after a competition in 1920, and Roith employed it for the public library several years later. Roith had been a pupil of Otto Wagner. He was employed largely by financial institutions, for whom he built some solid and sober banks, and by the municipality. The library interiors were refurbished by Ivo Oberstein and Jírí Zavadil in 1994–97.

Between the wars

131Bf **National Monument** 1926–30
U Památníku 1900, Žižkov
Jan Zázvorka and Jan Gillar

M Florenc

(Illustration page 100) A competition was organised in 1925 to design the National Monument for the top of Žižkov Hill, which was the site of a famous Hussite battle of 1420. The victorious Hussite commander, Jan Žižka of Trocnov, is commemorated in a bronze equestrian statue, designed by Bohumil Kafka and erected in 1950. The monument itself is an imposing granite-clad structure. The tall vertical section intersects a vault containing the grave of the unknown soldier and what used to be the 'Hall of the Soviet Army'. Political figures were also buried here – Klement Gottwald's body, for example, was displayed here after he died. The monument was enlarged in the 1940s and again in the 1950s, and several decorative features added inside and out.

The monument can be seen from almost anywhere in the city. The inner rooms are often open to the public. Below the monument, on the street which leads up the hill called U Památníku, is the Military Museum, designed in a similar manner by Zázvorka and Gillar at the same time as the monument.

132Bh **Barrandov Film Colony** 1931–34
Kříženeckého náměstí 5/322, Hlubočepy
Max Urban and Vladimír Grégr

M Smíchovské Nádraží, then B 246, 247, 248

The success of Czech film-making in the interwar period created the need for an out-of-town studio complex where open-air filming would be possible. The region known as Barrandov (named after the nineteenth-century French geologist, Barrande, who carried out geological research in the area) became known in the 1930s as a glamorous centre for the film industry. A group of developers led by Václav Havel invited architects to submit plans for a villa colony, and Max Urban was chosen to prepare the plan for the film studios and the nearby restaurant. Urban, a film-maker as well as an architect, planned the complex of studios to meet the technical needs of the new industry. The studio complex is unfortunately inaccessible to the public, but there is enough to see from the main square.

The **residential quarter** contains a number of notable Modernist villas for actors and other members of the film industry, including those by architects Houba, Stockar and Libra. Largely owing to the client's requests, the villas are an eclectic mix. For example, Vladimír Grégr's quirky, cottage-style Villa Pelc (Filmařská 4), is a piece of pure Hollywood romance.

Most of the villas are almost invisible because of the mature gardens that surround them, and can only be viewed at a distance. The best approach is to start at the film studios, and walk down the hill, following Lumiéru, then the pathway along Skalni to the terrace restaurant. Some of the villas visible around the hillside are listed at right.

Lumiéru:
41/181, 1932 *Max Urban.*
Barrandovská:
13/160, 1928–30 *Alois Houba.*
16/177, 1931–32 *Vladimir Grégr.*
20/190, 1932 *Vladimir Grégr.*
25/307, 1936 *Vladimir Grégr.*
29/385, 1937 *František Libra.*
46/180, 1931 *Vladimir Grégr.*
60/335, 1933–34 *Heřman Abeles, Leo Mayer.*
Skalní:
10/327, 1931–32 *Vladimir Grégr.*
17/172, 1931 *Rudolf Stockar.*
Filmařská:
3/336, 1934 *Jaroslav Fröhlich.*
4/337, 1934–35 *Vladimir Grégr.*
9/404, 1938–39 *Vilém Lorenc, Jan Čermák.*

133Bh Barrandov Terase Restaurant and Swimming Pool 1929–32

Barrandovská 1/165, Hlubočepy

Max Urban, Vladmir Grégr and Václav Kolátor

M Smíchovské Nádraží, then B 246, 247, 248

Further down the hill from the Barrandov Film Colony **132** is the Barrandov Terase Restaurant designed by Urban in 1927–29, with alterations made by Vladimír Grégr in 1939. The restaurant was conceived as a series of semi-circular terraces overlooking a swimming pool in the gorge below. The restaurant terraces lead on to gardens, now rather untended. The restaurant has a glazed dining hall and a lookout tower. The swimming pool, designed by Václav Kolátor, had a spectacular diving platform, and a dressing pavilion. Unfortunately, it is now disused, and the rusting remains of the diving platform is all that can be seen. The restaurant itself is still quite smart, although nowhere near as glamorous as it must have been in its early years – you are more likely to lunch with coach parties than with film stars.

134Bf Kostel Nejsvětějšího Srdce Páně (Church of the Sacred Heart) 1928–32

náměstí Jiřího z Poděbrad, Vinohrady

Josip Plečnik

M Jiřího z Poděbrad

This unusual building is unlike anything else in Prague, and seems to have more in common with the work of Michael Graves in the 1980s than it does with trends in Czech interwar architecture. Like his work at Prague Castle, the church is a myriad of references to various styles, as witness the simplified Neo-classical style of the cornice above the dark brick body of the building, with various Assyrian and Cubist references in the angular doorways. The slab-like tower is pierced through with a huge glass-faced clock, and flanked by Plečnik's trademark obelisks. Inside the church is a single nave, with a simple timber ceiling. The sculptures, depicting the Czech patron saints, are by artist Damián Pešan from designs by Plečnik himself.

Between the wars

135Ba **Baba Villa Colony** 1928–40
Dejvice
Pavel Janák and various architects

B 131

The Baba Villa Colony is the product of an architectural exhibition held in 1932 and organised by the Czechoslovak Decorative Arts Federation (*Svaz československého díla*), also known as the Czech Werkbund. The Werkbund was modelled on its Austrian and German counterparts, and the Baba estate was the last of the six Werkbund housing estates to be built in Europe. The first and best known, the Stuttgart Weissenhof estate of 1927, was an experiment in standardisation and new building technologies. It was intended as a prototype for a new form of living. The Brno branch of the Czech Werkbund organised a small-scale housing exhibition in 1928, *Nový Dům*, which was an example of collective housing. The Prague housing estate was proposed at that time, but by the time construction began its character had been significantly altered. Instead of collective housing and standardisation, the Baba estate is a range of 33 individual luxury villas. As Janák (who was responsible for the overall plan) stated in the programme's manifesto, the villas would 'provide an overview of what a one-family house can and should be, and how contemporary life dictates its layout, situation and size, lighting, heating, and the interior fixtures and fittings of individual rooms'. Many of the leading Czech Modern Movement architects, and only one foreign architect, Dutchman Mart Stam, designed villas for members of the Czech cultural and political élite. A few were designed as artists' studio homes, including Janák's own villa. Some villa plans were never realised, including contributions from Jaromír Krejcar and Adolf Loos. A few more radical proposals, including more minimal or standardised solutions (such as row housing) were also rejected. Baba's clients preferred the individuality and distinction of the bespoke villa to these views of a collective future. Client demands also led to many of the villas being constructed by more traditional methods than originally envisaged.

Czech architects excelled in the design of the modern villa prior to World War II. The Baba colony gave a number of young architects their first opportunity to see through a building scheme. The propensity of modern architects to only build luxury villas had its critics, such as Karel Teige. A number of the architects involved in Baba were designing (on paper only) experimental, standardised housing, and debating Functionalism and its social concerns in the architectural journals. The Baba project started out, a least, as a showcase for

Villa Herain

Villa Linda

Villa Palička

110

standardisation, but evolved into an estate of individual luxury dwellings. Janák's plan for the estate makes the most of its prominent position and wonderful views. Each villa has a substantial plot, and the houses are alternately sited at the front, then the back of the plot to allow for the maximum garden space around each one. Although the architects all found very individual solutions to the task set them, the villas share certain features: open planning, usually a single living space on the first or raised ground floor, roof terraces and balconies, and a garden aspect with services (bathrooms, kitchens, etc.) arranged on the street side of the building. Most houses were shown furnished during the exhibition, often with space-saving, built-in furniture designed by the architects. In total, 33 villas were built between 1932 and 1936, and a further five added to the estate in 1938–40. All are listed here, but several are worth mentioning individually. Mart Stam's villa for Jiří Palička is such a lightweight

construction of glass, steel and concrete that it appears made up of a series of intersecting screens. The glazed wall protecting the raised ground floor from the street shields a 'room' open to the garden. Oldřich Starý designed a studio house for artist Ladislav Sutnar, with built-in furnishings by Ladislav Žak. The largest villa on site in the Villa Suk, by Hana Kučerová-Záveská (one of the few women architects practising at the time), is a reinforced concrete frame building, with a cantilevered terrace on the garden side, and curved interior walls to soften the effect of the outer frame.

After 1948, some houses were converted into multi-family dwellings in line with Communist housing policy. Despite this, the estate has survived very well, with many villas cared for and preserved in their original state. More recently, residents have had to become used to the trail of architectural tourists visiting Baba.

Villa Mojžíš-Lom 1935–36, Na Babě 1/1783
Josef Gočár.
Villa Herain 1932, Na Babě 3/1782
Ladislav Žak.
Villa Bautz 1933, Na Babě 4/1799
František Kerhart.
Villa Balling 1932, Na Babě 5/1781
Hana Kučerová-Záveská.
Villa Linda 1933–34, Na Babě 6/1800
Pavel Janák.
Villa Heřman 1932, Na Babě 7/1780
Oldřich Starý.
Villa Moravec, 1933–34, Na Babě 8/1801
Vojtěch Kerhart.
Villa Palička 1932, Na Babě 9/1779, 1932
Mart Stam, Jiří Palička.
Villa Špíšek 1932–33, Na Babě 11/1777
Ladislav Machoň.
Villa Poláček 1932, Na Babě 12/1803
Jan E. Koula.
Villa Uhlíř 1932, Na Babě 13/1778
František Kavalir.
Villa Bělehrádek 1935–36, Nad Paťankou 24/1789
František Kerhart.
Villa Kytlica 1932–33, Nad Paťankou 22/1788
Josef Gočár.
Villa Maule 1932, Nad Paťankou 18/1786
Josef Gočár.
Villa Janák 1932, Nad Paťankou 16/1785
Pavel Janák.
Villa Glücklich 1933–34, Jarní 3/1798
Josef Gočár.
Villa Košťál 1933–34, Na Ostrohu 41/1791
František Kerhart.
Villa Dovodil 1932, Na Ostrohu 43/1797
Pavel Janák.

Villa Jiroušek 1932–33, Na Ostrohu 45/1796
František Kerhart.
Villa Bouda 1932, Na Ostrohu 46/1712
Oldřich Starý.
Villa Letošník 1932, Na Ostrohu 47/1795
František Kavalir.
Villa Joska 1932, Na Ostrohu 48/1711
Jaroslav & Karel Fišer.
Villa Suk 1932, Na Ostrohu 49/1794
Hana Kučerová-Záveská.
Villa Lisý 1932, Na Ostrohu 50/1710
Antonín Heythum, Evžen Linhart.
Villa Čeněk 1932, Na Ostrohu 51/1793
Ladislav Žak.
Three family house 1932, Na Ostrohu 52/1709
Oldřich Starý.
Villa Zadák 1934, Na Ostrohu 53/1792
František Zelenka.
Villa Zaorálek 1932, Na Ostrohu 54/1708
Ladislav Žak.
Villa Řezáč 1932, Na Ostrohu 56/1707
Vojtěch Kerhart.
Villa Peřina 1933, Na Ostrohu 58/1706
František Kerhart.
Villa Sutnar 1932, Průhledová 2/1790
Oldřich Starý.
Villa Lužná 1931–33, Průhledová 6/1804
Zdeněk Blažek.
Villa Munk 1932, Průhledová 10/1705
Josef Fuchs.
Matějská 7/1988, 1939–40 *Josef Grus.*
Matějská 9/1986, 1939–40 *Antonín Černý.*
Matějská 11/1877, 1939–40 *Antonín Kučera, Štěpán Zelenka.*
Matějská 13/1987, 1939–40, *Josef Grus.*
Matějská 17/1177, 1938–40 *Josef Grus.*
Matějská 19/1985, 1939 *František Kerhart.*

Between the wars

136Ag   Hotel Juliš 1928–33

Václavské náměstí 22/782, Nové Město

Pavel Janák

M Můstek

Janák had already designed a Cubist style café for the hotel proprietor on this site in the early 1920s. When Juliš approached him again to redesign the hotel, Janák showed how far he had come in adopting a definably Modernist approach. The arrangement of the building is much the same as other new hotels on Wenceslas Square – the hotel accommodation is above a public café, bar and shops on the ground floor, and there is a cinema in the basement. Aside from the wonderful night façade of the building (neon signs and back-lit glass), the building's modern character is most apparent in the café. Janák has squeezed the maximum amount of space out of the narrow building, creating a double-height bar with curved balcony and a huge window filling the whole of the front wall.

137Bi   Za Zelenou liškou Housing Complex 1930–38

U Nových Domů 1–111, Krč

František Libra, Jiří Kan and Antonín Černý

M Pankrác

From 1930, the Prague municipality organised a series of architectural competitions for the design of low-income apartment housing, to help alleviate the effects of the economic crisis upon both the poor and the building industry. This was the estate to be developed as a result of the 1930 competition. The blocks are all four to six storeys in height, some

with open corridor access (the solution suggested by Libra). The larger central blocks have communal stairwells instead of corridor access, and communal roof terraces. The blocks are planned around large green spaces, with children's play areas. Various architects contributed plans for the area. On the street, **Za Zelenou liškou** apartment buildings 2–14 were designed by Bohumír Kozák and Ladislav Kozák and built in 1932–33. On **U Nových Domů 1** Libra and Kan designed buildings 1–4, built in 1932–33. On **U Nových Domů 111**, Antonín Černý designed buildings 1–11, built in 1932–37.

138Ah Children's House 1925–29

Na příkopě 15/583, Nové Město

Ludvik Kysela

M Můstek

Originally built for the Praha Insurance Company, Kysela's first major Functionalist building demonstrates the direction his architecture was to take in the next few years. The building is divided up according to the function of its different floors. The office floors are indicated as separate from the lower part of the building and encased in a solid, white cube. The lower floors have long ribbon windows. Kysela was one of the group of architects associated with Karel Teige's journal, *Stavba*, who explored the possibilities of creating new, unprecedented building forms based on functional demands and new technical possibilities. In a few short years, he created several important commercial buildings, all glass-walled, skeletal structures, in the centre of Prague including the Bata Building 141, and then ceased working abruptly in the early 1930s, although he lived until 1960.

139Ag Lindt Department Store 1925–27

Václavské náměstí 4/773, Nové Město

Ludvik Kysela

M Můstek

The consumer boom of the later 1920s created a new demand for department stores and businesses keen to express their modernity through their premises. The Lindt store was the first in Wenceslas Square to do so in the language of Functionalism. Kysela uses a simple uniform grid plan, determined by the reinforced concrete structure, which allows for the glass front wall and the open passageway leading through to Jungmannova. Between the wide glass strips are sections of black opaque glass. The glass and steel roof rises in steps and then curves over, giving the building a rather mechanistic appearance. Kysela employs the same ground plan in the Bata Building 141.

Between the wars

140Ac Faculty of Law 1928–29

náměstí Curieových 9/701, Staré Město

Jan Kotěra and Ladislav Machoň

M Staroměstská; T 17, 51, 54

Kotěra had designed the Law Faculty of Charles University in 1914, but the plan was not carried out until 1928, when Machoň simplified the original design. The pantile roof and gable is typical of Kotěra – he used it to different, and more successful, effect on the Mozarteum **97**. The roofline and flattened façade give the building a feeling of old Prague but, as the building stands apart from the Old Town (on a prime site next to the river), this does not immediately register. In fact, it makes the building appear uncomfortably proportioned. The sculptures set into the gable are by B. Stefan.

141Ag Bata Department Store 1928

Václavské náměstí 6/774, Nové Město

Ludvik Kysela

M Müstek

Next door to the Lindt store **139**, built by the same architect in the previous year, is the central Prague store for the famous Moravian Bata Shoe company. The Bata (or Baťa) Company were well known for their patronage of modern architects in the interwar period, and had developed a large industrial town at Zlín, complete with worker housing, factory and administrative buildings and services all designed by their in-house architectural team. At Zlín, architect František Gahura had developed a module system of construction, based on a reinforced concrete frame structure of 6.15 square metre modules. This system, with either brick or glass infills or metal shuttering, was used for the construction of most of their multi-storey buildings, including the Prague department store. The store is eight storeys high, with a two storey basement. The façade of the building was entirely glass, with strips of white Opaxit glass to distinguish between each level. The interior plan was very open, but recent reconstruction has meant the loss of its original layout, in an effort to maximise the shop floor space. The glass façade has been renewed, but some of the original qualities of the building's appearance have been lost. From time to time the store holds small exhibitions about the Baťa company, which demonstrate the radical nature of the company's organisation in the interwar period. In some other Czech and Slovak towns, it is still possible to see the Baťa store – always a radical Modernist design, and usually as tall as the local officials would allow it to be. Kysela's work with the Baťa Company was as consultant rather than as part of their in-house team, and it is likely that he was approached on the strength of the Lindt project.

142Ag Alfa Building 1927–29

Václavské náměstí 28/785, Nové Město

Ludvik Kysela and Jan Jarolím

M Müstek

The Alfa complex, also named U Stýblů, is the last of the three commercial projects by Kysela in Wenceslas Square, built at the same time as the Bata Building **141**. It is constructed of reinforced concrete, with two vertical glass bays projecting from the main façade on Wenceslas Square. Inside, there is an arcade with a glass brick roof. Many of the small shop units in the arcade have retained their original appearance. At the time it was built, the Alfa contained the largest cinema in Prague.

143Bb Villa Gibian 1927–29

Charlese de Gaulla 22, Bubeneč

Jaromír Krejcar

M Dejvická

Designed for the entrepreneur, Gibian, Krejcar's villa demonstrates the mature purist architecture he had developed for the private residence. The Gibian villa follows on from his 1924 plans for writer Vladislav Vančura's villa in Zbraslav, which in turn shows the influence of Le Corbusier. In the Vančura villa, the services were separated from the living quarters, and the living area designed as a continuous set of interlinking spaces, without formal divisions. In the Gibian villa, the service area of the house is separated from the main living quarters, in a block on the north side of the plot. From this block the main house is accessed by means of a graduated ramp. The box-like volume of the house is broken up with a series of terraces and balconies on ground and first floor. The metal railings add to the building's nautical character. Krejcar extolled the virtues of the 'Architecture of the Transatlantic Steamliner' in an article published in *Život II* in 1923.

Between the wars

144Bh Villa Říha 1929–30

Nad Santoškou 1/1911, Smíchov

Josef Karel Říha

T 14

This property was designed as the architect's own family home. The street-facing wall is almost featureless, except for the thin bay window, which marks the staircase inside. The garden side is much more interesting, and looks on to spectacular views across the valley. Apart from the sun terraces on the roof, there is an outside 'room', partly enclosed by a curved frame, but with no walls or windows. Říha has employed all the typical 'streamlined' Modernist details on what is actually a relatively traditional family home.

145Be Villa Müller 1928–30

Nad hradnim vodojemem 14/642, Střešovice

Adolf Loos and Karel Lhota

T 1, 2, 18, 56

This is the most famous modern villa in Prague and the most eulogised; it is possibly the finest of Loos's career. Loos's two buildings for Prague – the other is the Winternitz Villa **150** – were designed late in his career, with assistance from the engineer, Karel Lhota. The Müller house is a masterpiece of complexity and quality. On the outside, the building is a plain, rather ugly box, which seems almost obsessive in its inaccessibility. Inside, the space 'unfolds' through a series of levels and steps, into sunnier and more spacious rooms as you climb through the building. The central stairwell is so planned as to practically allow access to every room in the house. There are no corridors, just a smaller informal room linking to another larger space. Walls and divisions are cut away, leaving shelves, seats or balustrades so that the view into the next space is always 'framed' in some way. The building is also a fine piece of craftsmanship – there are plenty of luxury materials and beautiful finishes, as always specified by Loos.

146Bf Church of St Wenceslas 1928–33
náměstí Svatopluk Čech, Vršovice
Josef Gočár

T 4, 22; B 124

Set on a dramatic raised platform, Gočár's church echoes the lie of the land as it rises in steps behind its slim central tower to a height of eighty metres. The lower building is a single span divided by two columns, which support the tower. Facing up the hill is a semi-circular presbytery of double height, with stained glass designed by Josef Kaplický, the father of London-based architect Jan Kaplický of Future Systems.

147Bf General Pension Institute 1929–34
náměstí Winston Churchilla 2/1800, 1839, 1840, Žižkov
Josef Havlíček and Karel Honzík

M Hlavni nádraží

The General Pension Institute organised a closed competition for the design of their new headquarters in 1928, which was won by two young architects in their twenties. Havlíček and Honzík proposed an unusual cruciform plan, with two addi-

tional wings branching from two of the central elements. The central cruciform section is eleven storeys high, with three-storey wings containing shops and flats. The building is of reinforced concrete with ceramic tile cladding, and the architects used a number of mass-produced elements, which proved to be very economical. The main staircases and lifts are located at the centre of the building. It is now the trade union headquarters. The building has the distinction of being the largest Functionalist project to actually be built in Prague in this period, and has been regularly written about since then.

148Ak Mánes Building 1928–30
Masarykovo nábřeží 1/250, Nové Město
Otakar Novotný

M Narodní třída

This extraordinary building (now a historic monument) was designed by Novotný for the Mánes Association of Artists. The association had been founded in 1887, named after the prominent Czech painter, Josef Mánes. Otakar Novotný had been the association's president since 1920 and had attempted to finance the building of these premises since 1923. After various modifications to the plan, and problems with funding, the building was begun in 1928. A location had been found on public land on the site of an old windmill, straddling the river. Novotný's solution to the site problem was to design

a piece of 'bridging' architecture, planned in three sections: the embankment side is a block used for exhibitions, the central 'bridge' contains the social functions (now a restaurant), and on the island side is a terraced café. The building is of a reinforced concrete construction. The supporting posts divide up the façade evenly, with glass infill. Sections of the flat roof are also glazed, so that the galleries and restaurant are top-lit.

The building is the only piece of isolated Modernist architecture in the historic town centre. Many slight modifications have been made since its completion, the first in 1932 when the island side of the building was extended. It still serves as an exhibition venue, and the terrace restaurant is a pleasant place to sit and eat in summer.

149An Villa Pick 1930–31
U Mrázovky 7/2071, Smíchov
Arnošt Wiesner

M Anděl; B 137, 508

The house is so overgrown with ivy that it is at first difficult to recognise its most interesting points. Wiesner's villa appears to be a cross between the turn-of-the-century artist-studio houses, inspired by the English Arts and Crafts Movement, and the early Viennese projects of Adolf Loos. The asymmetry of the façades and the humpbacked roof are close to Loos's Steiner house of 1910. Its picturesque character is a retreat from the severe Functionalism of domestic design at the time. The villa was modified by Eugene Rosenberg in 1938, in the year before he left to settle in London.

150An   Villa Winternitz 1931–32

Na Cihlářce 10/2092, Smíchov

Adolf Loos and Karel Lhota

M Anděl; B 137, 508

After the Villa Müller **145**, this is the second, and lesser known, building in Prague that had Loos's involvement. In reality, he largely supervised the work of his pupil Lhota here. Much less impressive than the Müller house, the Villa Winterniz is stepped at the back to allow for two or three terraces before reaching garden level. Like the Müller house, this villa has a basement level demarcated by the use of a different brick. It also has traditional, widely spaced windows, arranged much more symmetrically on the façade than Loos's other villa projects. It is now a kindergarten.

151Bb   French Schools 1931–34

Božkova 3/1784, Dejvice

Jan Gillar

M Dejvická

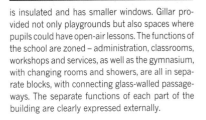

A number of radical designs for schools were produced in the 1920s and 1930s, which ignored traditional practices and instead looked to provide functional building complexes with maximum sunlight, suitable ventilation and insulation, as well as the most up-to-date facilities. The design for the French Schools in Dejvice was the most highly regarded of these, and was used subsequently as a model for other school designs in Prague. The competition-winning complex of buildings comprised a kindergarten, elementary school and what was originally a French grammar school. The most interesting feature of Gillar's design is the planning of the windows, with the large windows placed on the sunny side, while the other side of the building is insulated and has smaller windows. Gillar provided not only playgrounds but also spaces where pupils could have open-air lessons. The functions of the school are zoned – administration, classrooms, workshops and services, as well as the gymnasium, with changing rooms and showers, are all in separate blocks, with connecting glass-walled passageways. The separate functions of each part of the building are clearly expressed externally.

152Bc   Villa Hain 1932–33

Na vysočanských vinicích 31/404, Vysočany

Ladislav Žak

B 151, 181; T 8, 19

Žak built this villa for Miroslav Hain, a wealthy aircraft manufacturer, hence some of the rather quirky details. The roof has a tiny viewing platform, rather like a diving board, from which the owner could watch his planes take off from the nearby Kbely airfield. The house also has an incredible cantilevered sun terrace – a box-like projection from the front of the villa, which originally had fabric screens used to 'curtain off' the terrace. A steep,

Between the wars

railed ladder runs from the viewing platform down to the terrace. The space underneath the cantilevered terrace created another outdoor 'room' in the shade. The villa's situation, on a high jut of land on a steep hillside, was exploited by Žak to express his idea of the close relationship between built form and natural landscape. Its clever position, and the mature trees in the garden, make it difficult to get a full view of the villa from the road below, but must give full privacy to its inhabitants. The best way to approach the villa is by the steps up the hill from the bottom of Vysočanská, along the footpaths which crisscross what were once vineyard terraces.

153Be **Housing Estate** 1934–39

Mládeže & Nad Kajetánkou, Břevnov

Ladislav Machoň

T 8, 22; B 108, 174

This housing estate was planned by Machoň, with the eight individual tenement blocks designed by Antonín Černý, Václav Hilský, Rudolf Jasenský and Karel Koželka and built betweeen 1937 and 1939. The blocks are accessed by stairs. They are organised on a linear plan around communal gardens and a wide central avenue. Machoň's plan follows the contours of the hill, so that the blocks are arranged in a rather dynamic plan. Unlike some of the postwar, mass-housing projects, the interwar architects gave careful consideration to the provision of sunlight, ventilation and sanitary facilities.

154Ba **Villa Baarová** 1937

Neherovská 8/677, Dejvice

Ladislav Žak

B 125, 131

As with the villa he designed for film director Martin Frič – Villa Frič (1934–35) at Na lysinách 15/208, Hodkovičky (not included in the guide because of its inaccessibility) – Žak employed a poetic approach to the language of Functionalism on the Villa Baarová. The structure of this house is softened with curved corners, recessed balconies and the use of staircases to break up the solidity of the exterior. Žak's extensive use of a nautical vocabulary is apparent on many of his villa designs. Here they include a strange little funnel chimney and porthole windows. In all his villa designs, Žak consistently applied a metaphoric language of Modernism, conjuring up images of air, sea and speed. In this sense, he can be compared to Jaromir Krejcar, who also treated architecture as a 'system of signs', and from whom Žak took inspiration. This house was designed for the film actress Lída Baarová.

155Ah Živnostenská Bank 1936–38

Na příkopě 24–36, Nové Město

František Roith

M náměstí Republicky

The development of the historic city core into a major financial and administrative zone in the 1920s was largely handed over to a number of architects working in a modern classicist manner. These architects, of whom Roith was one, had all been pupils of Wagner in Vienna, and their monumental vision of the city found favour with wealthy banking firms and civic bodies. Roith's design for the most powerful of Czech banks, Živnostenská Banka, replaced a Neo-Renaissance building that was barely more than 30 years old. The sculpture by A. Popp that had adorned the old building was kept and repositioned at the centre of Roith's new granite-clad façade. The building was equipped with the

best technical services and furnished to a high standard. Some of the private offices apparently retain their original interiors, and the circular banking hall is still an impressive space. Although Roith's commission followed a competition, he probably seemed an obvious choice, as he had designed the State Savings and Investment Bank (42/796 Wenceslas Square) in a similar manner in 1926–31.

156Bb Zemská Bank Apartment Building 1936–37

náměstí Svobody 1/728, Dejvice

Richard Podzemný

M Dejvická

This apartment block, nicknamed 'the glass palace', was the winner of a competition organised by the Czech Provincial Bank. The apartments were rather more luxurious than some earlier housing projects of this type, and were particularly unusual for the careful provision made for the residents' gardens and roof terraces. The building is of a reinforced concrete frame construction, clad with ceramic tiles. It is arranged in two blocks: one rectangular seven-storey block with communal roof space and private balconies facing the square, and an elegantly curved six-storey corner block with balco-

nies set into the corner. The top storey is recessed to allow for wider balconies. Space for fifteen shop units was provided at street level. The interior of the entrance hall to the apartments is little altered. There is a central glass lift shaft. Underneath the shared courtyard garden at the rear of the building is an underground garage.

157Bb Secondary School 1937–38

Europská 33/330, Dejvice

Evžen Linhart

M Dejvická

This building is now a teacher-training college but was originally a secondary school. Linhart uses an L-shaped plan, seven storeys high, with a roof terrace and studio rooms on the top floor lit by an angled, glass wall. The school is neither as complex nor as elegant a solution as the nearby French Schools, designed by Jan Gillar **151**. Linhart's plan is much more compact, partly due to the restrictions of the site. Unlike Gillar's building, the exterior

of the college is more uniform, with little variation in fenestration to distinguish between the various functions within the building. The classrooms are lit by continuous window bands. The entrance and staircase are marked by a section of glass bricks. The building has recently been renovated.

Between the wars

158Ah Bílá Labut Department Store 1938–39
Na poříčí 23/1068, Nové Město
Josef Kittrich and Josef Hrubý

M náměstí Republicky

The Bílá Labut (or 'White Swan') department store is perhaps one of the finest Functionalist service buildings in Europe. It was constructed for the company Brouk & Babka. The building is designed around a central tower, with a huge glass grid façade made of thermolux and stainless steel bars, suspended above a recessed entrance floor. The entrance is divided by a series of five glass display cubes. The two-storey basement contains staff workrooms, storerooms and distribution facilities. There are nearly 10,000 square metres of retail space on the six floors above. The three storeys of the tower, behind a roof terrace, contain staff restaurant facilties and office space. All the original fittings and furnishings (some of which remain) were designed by Jan Gillar. The building was extended after World War II by a new wing connecting to Biskupská Street. It is very tatty inside now, and the exterior could do with renovation, but its current state does not hide the drama of the glass façade, hovering above ground level.

159Ac National Technical Museum 1938–40
Kostelni 42–44, Holešovice
Milan Babuška

M Vltavská; T 5, 12, 14, 17

The Association of the Technical Museums had been planning a purpose-built home for their collection, mainly acquired from international exhibitions, since their inception in 1910. An initial competition in 1935 resulted in the choice of Babuška as coordinating architect to plan two separate buildings for the museums of Agriculture and Technology. The former ceased to serve its original purpose in the 1950s. The museum buildings were to be part of a larger plan for the redevelopment of the area bordering Letná Plain. However, immediately after its completion in 1941, the new building was commandeered by the occupying German authorities. Only after the war were the museum's collections installed in the building.

The buildings are of strictly functional plan and appearance, except for the pared-down Classical entrance. The exterior is clad with stone on the lower storeys. The Technical Museum has three four-storey wings (with a double basement), which house smaller linear galleries. Behind the centre wing is the huge, single-span 'Transportation Hall', four storeys high, with viewing galleries around the walls. The museum's collections represent the major industrial and technical achievements of Czechoslovakia, including early Tatra and Škoda vehicles. There are also regular exhibitions of twentieth-century Czech industrial design. The site is designated a historical landmark, for its architectural and town-planning importance.

From annexation to independence 1939–89

60Bh **Prague-Smíchov Railway Station** 1947–56

Nádražní 1/279, Smíchov

Jan Zázvorka and Ladislav Žak

M Smíchovské Nádraží

The main railway station at Smíchov was first built in the early 1860s to serve this growing industrial region along the river. The area surrounding the station still retains many nineteenth-century factory buildings, including the nearby Staropramen Brewery complex, also on Nádražní. In the early 1950s, the station was enlarged according to plans drawn up by Žak and Zázvorka. Zázvorka was also the architect of the earlier 'National Monument' on Žižkov Hill **131**. The two buildings are very similar in

style, using the same severe geometric masses. The façade of the railway station has been partially covered up by alterations and the addition of a canopy, but its general form is still recognisable.

61Bb **Planetarium** 1952–62

Výstaviště Exhibition Site, Bubeneč

Jaroslav Fragner

M Nádraží Holešovice; T 5, 12, 17

The planetarium was added to the complex of entertainment buildings on the Exhibition Site **64** in the early 1960s, although Fragner's designs date from 1952. In this year, the site was designated the Julius Fučik Park of Culture and Rest, named after the Communist writer who had been executed by the Nazis. There is a grace about Fragner's use of Classical forms here that is missing from so many state-approved architectural projects of the 1950s. The Planetarium has a circular ground plan, with a curved colonnade entrance, featuring thin, light columns. The auditorium is in the dome, in which images of the night sky are projected. The Planetarium runs popular science programmes and events, as well as concerts. Fragner's building was one of a number of additions to the exhibition site during the 1950s and 1960s, including the Expo 58

Restaurant **165** and the Czech Pavilion from the 1958 Brussels Expo, both designed by František Cubr, J. Hrubý and Z. Porkorný and re-erected on its present site in 1960.

From annexation to independence

162Bb Hotel International 1952–57
Koulova 15/1501, Dejvice
František Jeřábek

M Dejvická; T 20, 25

The International is one of the most extraordinary and disconcerting buildings of the Czech Communist era. Jeřábek's design was carried out by workers from the Military Design Institute. It was intended for the military and visiting Soviet officials. The building uses a model common in Stalinist countries of the period – the official style of Socialist Realism, which was a combination of stripped Classicism and so-called 'peoples' detailing'. The building is decorated with friezes and reliefs that relate to historical and mythological tributes to Prague, as well as sgraffito decoration and caryatids, with a great deal of ersatz historical decoration inside.

Two six-storey wings branch from the central fourteen-storey tower. From the entrance hall leading towards the courtyard at the back there is a low wing containing restaurants and function rooms. Once inside, the sense of grandeur is lost – too much has been crammed into the (considerable) space, the ceilings are low, and the entrance halls and corridors badly proportioned. It caters now mainly for business people and coach parties, although with a little imagination it could be turned into the first 'socialist experience' theme-park hotel.

163AI Hotel Jalta 1954
Václavské náměstí 45/818, Nové Město
Antonín Tenzer

M Muzeum

This is a rather more restrained example of Socialist Realist hotel architecture in comparison to the Hotel International 162. The symmetrical façade is decorated with travertine marble facing, simple mouldings and caryatids. All the hotel rooms are oriented towards the square, some with balconies – in other hotels on the square the rooms do not overlook it, but are situated instead at the back of the building. Inside the Jalta, on the raised ground floor with its terrace café, there is an impressive curved staircase.

64Bb Czech Technical University 1957–70

Dejvice

Various architects

M Dejvická

The site for the Czech Technical University, to one side of Vítězné náměstí, had initially been developed between the wars according to a plan by Antonín Engel. A public competition for its completion was organised in 1957, and the winners were František Novák and Gustav Paul. The first stage of development, between 1958 and 1960, resulted in the two blocks housing the Faculties of Mechanical and Electrical Engineering on Technická. The Faculties of Civil Engineering and Architecture were built along Thákurova from 1964–70 by Gustav Paul, František Čermák and Jaroslav Paroubak. Two rectangular blocks, of seven and fourteen storeys, were built perpendicular to each other. They are connected by a two-storey entrance wing, which has an atrium. The two masses that project from the Faculty of Civil Engineering are lecture theatres. At the back of the complex, bordering Bíla Street, are a number of workshops and laboratories. The Faculty of Architecture is in the tallest wing, and is generally unpopular as it is an uncomfortable building to work in.

165Ad Restaurant Praha Expo 58 1958

Letenské sady, Letná

František Cubr, J. Hrubý and Z. Porkorný

M Vltavská; T 5, 12, 14, 17

The restaurant built for the World Expo' held in Brussels in 1958 was subsequently re-erected on this site on Letná Plain, with a magnificent view over the city and the river. Its partner exhibition pavilion, designed by the same architects, was similarly moved to Prague to form part of the Výstaviště exhibition site **64, 161**. The restaurant is an impressive and lightweight glass and steel semi-circular structure, above a low and recessed ground floor. The building stresses its modernity as well as its portability, and must have been a refreshing architectural choice for the Expo' in comparison with the more bombastic examples of Czech architecture from the early 1950s. In fact, by 1956, the rejection of the 'cult of Stalin' in Socialist countries triggered a revival of interest in Functionalist architecture. The Expo buildings are fine examples of the con-

tinuation of Modern movement ideas, as well as a sign that Czech architects were, of course, well aware of western postwar architectural concerns.

Very sadly, the restaurant has fallen into disuse and disrepair, and despite attempts to save it, its fate remains unknown. From a distance, the original signage on the terrace wall in front is still so bold, it is a surprise to find it empty. It is not possible to ascertain whether the interior decoration, including wall and ceiling painting by Fišárek and his pupils, are still intact.

From annexation to independence

166Bc Invalidovna Housing Estate 1959–65
Molákova & Za invalidovnou
Josef Polák and the Prague Design Institute
M Invalidovna

The Invalidovna estate is an early experimental housing project designed by a group of architects headed by Josef Polák. On a site of 13 hectares were planned facilities for 4,000 inhabitants, including blocks of five to eleven-storey flats. It is rather like the English Alton East Estate in Roehampton, London – mixed development amid mature landscaping. The buildings are constructed of six-metre span panels. The nature of construction and the planning of the district were later seen as a blueprint for larger, more impersonal and, ultimately, less suc- cessful housing projects in the later 1960s. In one corner of the estate is the Hotel Olympik (Sokolovská 138), also designed by Polák and his team of architects in 1967–71. It is still a pleasant location, and has the feel of a successful community plan, unlike many of the other estates that followed.

167Bh Pankrác Housing Estates I, II & III 1962–68
Various architects
M Pankrác, Budejovicka

This vast housing suburb was the result of a competition organised in the early 1960s. As the housing crisis in Prague reached a peak, a government initiative prompted the development of massive residential quarters on the edge of the city. Pankrác was the largest estate of its time, until the 'new town' developments of the later 1960s were underway. It was planned as two centres, comprising Pankrác I (2,000 flats for over 7,000 inhabitants) and Pankrác II (1,400 flats for 5,000 inhabitants). The competition-winning architects of this first stage were Jindřich Krise and Luděk Todl, coordinated by J. Ladovský. In the later 1960s, a third centre was added, Pankrác III, which was completed in 1968. Each section is divided into three housing areas, planned as a communal centre with schools and playgrounds. The residential blocks are variously four, eight and twelve storeys high. Situated on the plain between the Nusle, Michle and Krc valleys, the estates are bleak, windswept, dirty and dusty in summer. The communal green spaces have been all but abandoned; they are now overgrown and unkempt. The estates are served by two metro stations and a network of buses.

168Ai Spartakiad Stadium Complex 1930–78
Vaníčkova, Břevnov
Various architects
B 132, 143, 149

The popularity of mass Socialist sporting events created the need for the rebuilding and extension of the existing sports ground on Strahov Hill. After 1948, sports complexes previously paid for by Czech sports clubs and associations came under central state control. From 1955 onwards, the huge stadium became the venue for the national 'Spartakiads' – mass events that served as political rallies as well as sporting displays. The first buildings for the central Sokol stadium were erected in 1930, by a team of architects led by Alois Dryak.

Other smaller stadia were added, including an army stadium to the north of the complex. After 1948, concrete grandstands were added. The east stand, with its glass viewing platform, was added in the late 1960s. The whole complex was subsequently enlarged to include a student 'village' on the eastern section of the site, comprising 11 student hostels, as well as various service buildings, dining rooms and a health centre. In 1978, the Evžen Rošický Sports stadium was redesigned for the European Athletics Championships, named after a Communist athlete and journalist who had been executed by the Nazis. It was designed by Petr Kutnar and Svatopluk Zeman.

169Bh Podolí Swimming Stadium 1960–65
Podolská 74/43, Podolí

Richard Podzemný

T 3, 17

Far south along the Vltava embankment is this swimming sports complex designed by Podzemný in collaboration with Gustav Kuchař and Juraj Domič in 1960. The site of a former quarry was chosen for this stadium planned for large public events. There is an indoor pool, the roof of which forms the stadia seating for the two outdoor pools behind it. The seating stand, with enough space for 4,500 spectators, forms the distinctive wave-shaped profile of the building.

170Al Federal Assembly 1966–73
Vinohradská 1/52, Nové Město

Karel Prager

M Muzeum

Stranded on a traffic island between the Smetana Theatre and the National Museum is the home of the National Parliament. The original building on this site was the Stock Exchange, designed by Jaroslav Rössler in 1936–38, which in the postwar period was a relic of a banished economic system. The Federal Assembly was moved into the Stock Exchange on a temporary basis, until a competition was organised to redevelop the site to its new purpose in 1965. Prager's suggestion was to create a new superstructure above the old building, squashing it beneath a huge steel and glass cage, which is supported on vast stilts. The result is an ugly and ungainly building that repels visitors rather than attracts them. The fate of the old building, dwarfed

uncomfortably by the new, appears now as an unfortunate symbol of the postwar political system. There are several sculptural works around the building, including a steel pylon representing *Czechoslovak Statehood* and a work by Vincenc Makovský that came from the Czechoslovak Pavilion at the 1958 Brussels Expo entitled *Nuclear Age*.

From annexation to independence

171Ao Church of St Emmaus (Na Slovanech)
1965–68

Vyšehradská 49/320, Nové Město

František M. Černý and Vladimír Kamberský

M Karlovo náměstí; T 18, 24

The modern tower of this church, designed as two intersecting concrete wings, forms an impressive contrast to the ancient Benedictine monastery 9, known as Na Slovanech, meaning 'At the Slavs'. In February 1945, the church was heavily damaged during an Allied bombing raid. Restoration work began the year after, and continued into the late 1950s, when a competition was organised to come up with an architectural scheme that would harmonise the remaining ancient buildings and some nearby modern development. Černý's bold design was the eventual winner, once it had been established that a modern solution was not necessarily out of keeping with the surroundings. The two crossing shells of the tower are of reinforced concrete. They were meant to emulate the original Gothic gable as well as the twin Baroque towers, which had been added in the seventeenth century. The tower is an elegant and effective solution when seen from a distance, but this effect is rather lost up close.

172Ac Hotel Intercontinental 1967–74
Pařížská 30/43, Staré Město

Karel Bubeníček, František Cubr, Karel Filsak and Jan Šrámek

M Staroměstská

The hotel was described at the time of its construction as an attempt to integrate modern architecture with the historic Old Town, although it is difficult to see why, as it dwarfs the surrounding buildings. It is a huge L-shaped block topped by a large slab, which forms the panoramic restaurant. The vertical window sections on the façades are interposed with sections of rough concrete and some ceramic decoration. The recessed ground floor is dark and anonymous. The interiors are decorated with specially-commissioned art works. Extremely luxurious when it first opened, the hotel still aims for the upper tourist and business bracket. It was designed with full conference facilities and a number of expensive bars and cafés. However, the roof-top restaurant does give the best views of the whole of Josefov, providing the best way of understanding the modern planning of this part of the town.

173Ah Kotva Department Store 1971–75
náměstí Republicky 8/656, Nové Město

Věra Machoninová and Vladimir Machonin

M náměstí Republický

This is Prague's busiest department store, which now has franchises for most leading western brandnames in clothing, cosmetics and domestic ware. The store is designed as a cluster of hexagonal sections of reinforced cast concrete supported by pillars. The clusters project unevenly into the street, forming a canopied walkway at street level and a number of entrance openings. The exterior is clad with panels of brown aluminium and glass with thin alloy parapets and some exposed concrete sections. Orientation inside the building is quite easy,

and it is surprisingly pleasant, although always crowded. There are four shopping floors and a top restaurant floor. Hidden away in the triple basement are service rooms and a large car park.

174Bi Domov Furniture Store 1972–81
Budějovice náměstí, Pankrác
Věra Machoninová

M Budějovická

The huge, out-of-town home furnishings store was once the state-run 'Domov'. Now it is occupied by the popular Swedish firm IKEA. Věra Machoninová was also responsible for the Kotva department store 173 in the city centre. Both stores demonstrate a different solution to the problem of circulation. This store has a steel framework supporting six floors, and the whole block is 'stepped' in the middle, with a central well containing stairs and escalators. The building sits on a complicated system of concrete terraces and walkways, which connect to the nearby metro station. The building is partially clad in metal sheeting with horizontal strip windows.

175Ak Máj Department Store 1973–75
Národní 26/63, Nové Město
John Eisler, Miroslav Masák and Martin Rajnik (SIAL)

M Národní třída

This was originally the Máj department store, then was taken over by the US company K-Mart, and is now owned and run by Tesco. The architects were members of the SIAL studio (Association of Engineers and Architects from Liberec), an innovative practice founded in 1968. Although the practice only formally lasted 3 years, SIAL still works as a loose association of creative architects and engineers. The Máj project represented their most significant work in Prague up to that point, planned as a conscious continuation of the Czech Functionalist tradition. In many respects, it is a high-tech building, making conscious use of an industrial aesthetic in the manner of, say, the Centre Pompidou. SIAL designed this in conjunction with the Swedish construction firm ABO. At this time, Swedish firms dominated foreign commercial construction in the city. The design is simple yet striking, although not ideally suited to the site. The façade on Národní is

clad in opaque white glass with continuous window strips at the top and bottom. This façade wraps around the corner of the building, but then gives way to a harsh exposed concrete cladding on the Spálená Street façade, which is rather unforgiving. The building overhangs the street along Národní, so that one is drawn into the open entrance and into the shop's traffic as one tries to walk past. At the rear of the building, overlooking the pedestrianised area surrounding Národní třída metro station is a glazed escalator tower, which gives the building more animation. The interior plan is simplified in the extreme, featuring large open warehouse spaces divided by temporary shop fittings.

From annexation to independence

176Be **Koospol Foreign Trade Association Building**
1974–77

Europská 178, Vokovice

Vladimir Fencl, Stanislav Franc and Jan Novácek

T 2, 26

The Koospol building is designed as a huge cube, raised over 11 metres from the ground on a pedestal so that it looks as if it rotates. The exterior of the building is clad in precast concrete elements. The ornamental features in the landscaped garden are also concrete. The cube itself is five storeys high, measuring 60 metres by 60 metres, built of reinforced concrete, and supported on four columns. Underneath the cube is a two-storey block, which contains the entrance hall and service and restaurant facilities. The atrium of the building has been dramatically landscaped, with water features and built elements adorned with greenery. The building can accommodate over 1,000 employees, and has recently been sold to an Austrian firm.

177Bh **Palace of Culture** 1975–80

Května 65/1640, Nusle

Jaroslav Mayer, Josef Karlík and Antonín Vanék

M Vyšehrad

Of all the grand architectural civic projects in the 1970s, this is perhaps the most insensitive addition to the urban environment. The Palace of Culture, or Congress, as it was alternatively known, provides a location for conferences, concerts and other large social or civic events. In 1975, a closed competition was organised, and the winning project submitted by the team of architects from the Military Design Institute led by Mayer, Karlík and Vanék. They proposed an irregularly shaped single block, three storeys high, built on a platform and facing towards the city centre. On the city side are viewing terraces and galleries. The asymmetrical exterior is designed so as to clearly reflect the planned functions of the interior. However, the huge mass of the palace

dominated this section of the city, dwarfing any other distinctive landmarks, its ugly solidity made uglier in contrast to the gracious spires and towers around it. It is also on a site too far out of the city for it to become an important cultural centre. If you do visit the building, it contains a large collection of fine and applied arts commissioned from a broad selection of leading contemporary artists. Much of this collection is on display in rooms not open to the general public.

178Ag ČKD Building 1975–83

Na příkopě 1/388, Staré Město

Alena Šrámková and Jan Šrámek

M Můstek

This is the administrative headquarters of the engineering company, Českomoravská Kolben Daněk, and also contains a public nightclub on the top floor and a café on the ground floor. The building is of steel clad with stone. It has a glass-walled corner section and three box-like windows, which project from the façade on the first floor. The architects have attempted to create a modern building that would emulate the *moderne* buildings on Wenceslas Square and Na příkopě. The architects' 'contextualist' approach to the site is one of the reasons for the building being described as the first Postmodern building in Prague. The glass clock tower echoes the roof line of Joseph Zasche's Viennese Union Bank opposite. Incorporated into the building is the entrance to Můstek metro station, designed by Jarmil Srpa and Zdeněk Volman.

179Af Malostranská Metro Station 1979

Klárova, Malá Strana

Zdeněk Drobný and Otakar Kuča

M Malostranská

The first proposal for an underground subway system in the centre of Prague was made in 1926 by two engineers, Vladimír List and Bohumil Belada. The municipal council eventually ordered plans to be drawn up in 1939, but work was cut short by the intervention of the German authorities two years later. However, after the war and until the 1960s, the favoured plan was for a tram system that would run mainly above ground, with only a small proportion below ground. Construction began in 1965, only to be halted when the plans were changed to an underground railway system in 1967. The metro consists of three lines. The first, from Karlín to Pankrác (Line C), opened in 1974; the second, from Vinohrady to Dejvice (Line A), opened in 1978; and the third, from Karlín to Smíchov (Line B), opened in 1985. All three lines have subsequently been extended to the outer suburbs and to the New Town developments. Further extensions are planned. The coordinating architect for Line C was Jaroslav Otruba, and for Lines A and B, Evžen Kyllar. The distinctive orientation map was designed by Jiří Rathousky. Inside the ticket halls and on the platforms there is evidence of a consistent visual identity. Some halls are decorated with ceramic tiles and highly coloured aluminium cladding, others with textured glass bricks. As a whole, the metro system is bright, clean and efficient.

The design of each station is dependent upon the above ground surroundings. Malostranská station, on Line A, is one of those stations with a distinctive above ground character, which nevertheless blends well with the historic surroundings. It was built on the site of an old exhibition pavilion, and is adjacent to the Valdštejn Gardens 23 and the Riding School Art Gallery. The entrance building is a narrow, glass-walled rectangle, with the escalators at one end and a small outdoor café at the other. The building is set into an attractive and much-used water garden, designed by Kuča, which borders the Riding School. The sculptures in the garden and on the walls of the station vestibule give the feeling that the station and garden are an extension of the art gallery.

180Ak   Nová Scéna (National Theatre Extension)
1980–83

Národní 4/1493, Nové Město

Karel Prager

M Národní třída

In the 1930s, proposals had been made to extend the premises of the original National Theatre building **58**. The plot surrounding the old theatre, between Národní and Ostrovní, was designated to accommodate new administrative and technical buildings in 1962. The competition to develop this area was won by Bohuslav Fuchs, one of the leading Functionalists of the Brno School in the 1930s. However, Fuchs died before work began, and the project was taken over by Pavel Kupka from the State Institute for Renovation of Historic Towns and Buildings (SURPMO), who designed the administration blocks. The design of the second theatre, called the Nová Scéna (New Stage), was entrusted to Karel Prager of Prague's Institute of Construction. Looking at Prager's building now, it is difficult to understand the rationale behind the design. The building is a heavy block, raised to create an open walkway underneath, and set back from the street so as not to interfere with the streetscape. The roofline is angled inwards at the top, to echo the proportions of the original theatre. It is clad with glass bricks, manufactured by the Bohemian Kavalier Glassworks. This cladding is supposed to catch the reflections of the façades of the surrounding older buildings, but it is hardly a sympathetic addition.

Architecture since 1989

Entrance to site

Outdoor auditorium

181Bb **Výstaviště Exhibition Site** 1990–91

U Výstaviště, Bubeneč

Various architects

M Nádraží Holešovice; T 5, 12, 17

For the centenary celebrations of the Jubilee Exhibition site **64**, a new group of buildings was added
in preparation for the 1991 Exhibition. In particular,
a new structure by Michal Brix was added at the rear
of the main 1891 Exhibition Hall. The white-painted
steel structure provides an outside auditorium arranged around a stage and light fountain, with a
series of walkways above the raked seating. The
steel towers, with their portholes and flagpoles, give
the site a nautical air. Other additional buildings

Exhibition Hall

provide extra indoor exhibition space, such as the
blue glass pyramid to the side of the main hall.

182Ab **Hotel Hoffmeister** 1990–93

Chotkova, Malá Strana

Petr Keil

M Malostranská

At first glance, this appears to be a reconstruction
of a complex of eighteenth-century buildings, perhaps a stableblock. In fact, it is a peculiar example
of the naive application of Postmodernism to a
small, prime site hotel. The building is cramped in
its space, and Keil has used a range of ill-matched
architectural references to create a rather incoher-
ent building, brightened with ice-cream colours.

Architecture since 1989

183Ag   **Office Building** 1992
Liliová 4/250, Staré Město
Jaroslav Šafer

M Staroměstská

This is a very sensitive and striking conversion of a Renaissance house and courtyard into an office complex. The glass stair tower that has been added in the corner creates a high-tech entrance to the building and enlivens the blank façade of the main building, which was added in the 1920s. Although private, you can enter the courtyard during business hours. However, it is best seen at night when the building is lit up to full effect.

184Ak   **Rašin Building** 1993–94
Rašínovo Nábřezi 80, Nové Město
Frank Gehry and Vlado Milunic

M Karlovo náměstí; T 3, 17

Gehry and Milunic's project for this prime site near the centre of the city is the most publicised Czech building of recent years. The site has remained empty since a stray US bomb destroyed the former building in 1945. Yugoslavian architect Milunic had become involved with a project to redevelop the site in the mid 1980s, when he was remodelling Václav Havel's apartment in the block next door to the empty site. His initial project concentrated on the dynamic relationship between two forms – something that was carried forward into the collaborative project with Gehry. After the revolution of 1989, the redevelopment of the site took on a new symbolic aspect, located next to the home of the new president. It is a focal point on the river embankment and one of only two bomb damage sites in the city centre from World War II. The new Dutch investors, Nationale Nederlanden argued for the involvement of a prominent western architect, and Gehry was chosen as the result of the closed competition.

The architects have drawn from a range of architectural forms to create a building both startling in aspect but sympathetic to the cityscape. The two towers, nicknamed Ginger and Fred, form the protruding corner – a common element on Prague city street intersections. The glass tower leans towards and twists around the boxlike concrete tower, and the 'skirts' of the glass tower billow out, supported on a mass of wavy treelike columns. The dynamic form of the building, with its tower tipped on its axis, appears to pay homage to Tatlin's Monument to the 3rd International. The top of the building is adorned with a twisted metal cupola. The river façade maintains the rhythmn of the nineteenth-century buildings on the embankment.

The building includes business accommodation, an auditorium and an exclusive top-floor restaurant. The ground floor is partly open and there is a little café there. The top three storeys have been occupied by Andersen Consulting, who commissioned Eva Jiricna to design the interiors for them. Jiricna adhered to Gehry and Milunic's building concept, dividing the space with glass partitions so as to leave the design intentions clear.

85Be Family Houses 1992–93

Loutkarska 6, Břevnov

Vlado Milunic

T 8, 22; B 191

These are two family houses, planned as two inter-locking hexagonals, with a shared terrace space between. Milunic uses references to earlier domestic building types and his interest in late Baroque architecture, particularly the work of Santini-Aichl, is given free rein here. It is a very different direction from Milunic's Neo-Functionalist projects of the 1970s and 1980s, such as the old people's home in Bohnice, designed in partnership with Jan Linek.

186Ad Praha City Centre Building 1993–95

Klimentská 46, Josefov

Otto Dvořák

M náměstí Republicky

The Viennese architect, Dvořák, designed the building for the company, European Property Development, in an attempt to remain sensitive to the scale and plan of its immediate vicinity. The form of the building is certainly deferential to its neighbours. Its bulk is lessened by the recessing of the uppermost storey and the window line and scale is in keeping. However, the brash use of materials and finishes means that the building announces its commercial status a little too loudly in what is largely a residential area.

187Ah Myslbek Building 1995–96

Na příkopě, Nové Město

Zdeněk Hölzel and Jan Kerel

M Müstek

The development of this site has a long history. Originally cleared in the early 1920s, an architectural competition winner in 1926 failed to be built. A new competition in 1988 was won by Hölzel and Kerel, but building work did not begin until the late 1990s. The building comprises a huge shopping galleria, which connects Na příkopě with Ovochý trh. This has a public, balconied mezzanine, and offices on the floors above. However, many compromises to the designs were made before construction began, and what has been built is an ungainly and unpopular addition to the city centre. It is sad, when reflecting on the city's recent history, that such ill-fitting projects can be built even now. The glass frontage on Na příkopě is insensitive and dwarfs the surrounding buildings. The Ovochý trh façade is much more subtle. The building has attracted major clients, such as the British stores, Marks & Spencer and Next Retail Ltd.

Selected bibliography

Obec architectktů Praha, *Česká Architectura, 1945–95*, Prague, Society of Czech Architects, 1995

Angelo Maria Ripellino, *Magic Prague*, trans. D. N. Marinelli, London, Macmillan, 1994

Ctibor Rybár, *Jewish Prague: Notes on History and Culture*, Prague, TV Spektrum, 1991

Vladimír Šlapeta, *Praha, 1900–1978: Průvodce po moderní Architektuře*, Prague, Národní Technické Muzeum, 1978

Jaroslava Staňková, Jíří Štursa and Svatopluk Voděra, *Prague: Eleven Centuries of Architecture*, trans. Z. Vyplel & D. Vaughan, Prague, PAV Publishers, 1992

Rostislav Švachá (ed.), *Devetsil: Czech Avant-Garde Art, Architecture and Design*, Oxford and London, Museum of Modern Art and the Design Museum, 1990

Rostislav Švachá, *The Architecture of the New Prague, 1895–1945*, Cambridge, Mass., MIT Press, 1995

Petr Wittlich, *Prague Fin de Siècle*, Paris, Flammarion, 1992

Author's acknowledgements

The author would like to thank the following institutions and individuals: The British Academy, Camberwell College of Arts (The London Institute), David Crowley, Matthew Frost, Eve Graves, Paul Greenhalgh, Michael Horsham, Pavla Hroudova, Milos Hrouda, Mílena Lamarová, Lauren MacAllister, Vlado Milunic, The National Technical Museum (Prague), Gillian Naylor, Ivo Oberstein, Milada Obersteinová, Daphne Pavitt, John Pavitt, Katherine Reeve, Radomíra Sedláková, Vladimir Slapeta, the University of Brighton, the Victoria and Albert Museum, Christopher Woodward, Jíří Zavadil, Elena Zavadilová, and especially Tim Burne.

Photographs

All photographs are by the author.

Index

Index

D–K

Hanavský Pavilion (1891), **66**
Hanuš of Mühlheim, 16
Harlas, František, 83
Hausknecht, Heinrich, **47**
Havel, President Václav (b. 1936), *27*, 1, 184
Havel, Václav, **90**, 132
Havlíček, Josef (1899–1961), *24*, **147**
Havlíček, Milan, 87
Heerman, Paul, 32
Heibl, Johann, 30
Herbst, František, 104
Herčik, František, 74
Hergesel, František, 64
Heythum, Antonín, (1901–54) 135
Hieser, Otto, **66**
High Synagogue (1577), 6
Hilbert, Kamil (1869–1933), 13
Hillger, H., 11
Hilský, Václav, 153
Hitler, Adolf (1889–1945), *25*
Hladova zed' (1360–62), **12**
Hlahol Choir Building (1903–6), **84**
Hlava Institute of Pathology (1913–21), **102**
Hlávka, Josef (1831–1908), **54**, 84
Hlávka Bridge (1909–11), **94**
Hlávka Students' Hostel, 84
Hlavní nádraží (1901–9), **80**
Hobza, Michal, 74
Hodek, František, 106, 107
Hodek block, 107
Hoffmann, Josef (1870–1956), 99
Hofman, Vlastislav (1884–1964), *21*, *22*, **109**
Hofmann, Karel, 110
Höhnel, Franz, 49
Hölzel, Zdeněk, **187**
Honzík, Karel (1900–66), *23*, *24*, **147**
Hotel Central (1898–1900), **76**
Hotel Hoffmeister (1990–93), **182**
Hotel Intercontinental (1967–74), **172**
Hotel International (1952–57), **162**, 163
Hotel Jalta (1954), **163**
Hotel Juliš (1928–33), **136**
Hotel Olympik (1967–71), 166
Houba, Alois, 132
House at the Black Madonna (1911–12), **104**, 110
House at the Green Lobster (1720s), 36
House at the Red Lion (1720s), 36
House of the Artists (1876–84), **60**
House of the Lords of Kunštát and Poděbrady (c. 1150–1250), **4**
House of the White Unicorn (c. 1562), **20**
housing estate (1934–39), **153**
Howard, Ebenezer (1850–1928), 119
Hrabě, Libra, 125
Hradčanská Radnice (1601–4), **22**
Hradčany, *7*, *8*
   Sternberg Palace (1698–1707), **31**
   Town Hall (1601–4), **22**
Hrubý, Antonín, 64
Hrubý, Josef, **158**, 161, **165**
Hurtig, Alfred, **63**
Hunger Wall (1360–62), **12**

Hus, Jan (1372–1415), *10*, 16
Hussite Wars, *10*
Hvězda Palace (1555–56), **21**

Industrial Palace (1891), **65**
Invalidovna House (1731–37), **37**
Invalidovna housing estate (1959–65), **166**

Jäckel, M. (1655–1738), 11, 29
Jagiellon dynasty, *10–11*
Janák, Pavel (1882–1956), *20–1*, *22*, *23*, 1, 7, 19, 26, **94**, 114, **115**, 119, 120, **123**, **135**, **136**
Jarolím, Jan, **142**
Jaroš, Tomáš, 19
Jasenský, Rudolf, 153
Jech, František, *26*
Jeřábek, František, **162**
Jewish cemetery, *17*
Jewish ghetto, *16–17*, 63
Jiráska, Alois (1851–1930), 21
Jiricna, Eva (b. 1939), 184
John, King of Luxembourg, 7
Josef II (1741–90), *13*, *14*
Josefov, *7*, *16–17*
   redevelopment (1893 onwards), 6, **63**
Joseph II, 1
Jubilee Exhibition (1891), *16*, **64**
Judith Bridge (1158–60), *9*, 11, 29
Jungling, Antonín, **51**
Jurkovič, Dušan (1868–1947), **89**

Kafka, Bohumil (1878–1942), 87, 115, 119, 131
Kafka, Franz (1883–1924), 1
Kamberský, Vladimír, **171**
Kan, Jíří, **137**
Kaňka, František M. (1674–1766), 10, 26, 30
Kaplický, Jan, 146
Kaplický, Josef, 146
Karlík, Josef, **177**
Karlín development (1817–), *15*, **48**, 96
Kateřína, Princess, of Lobkowicz, 40
Kavalir, František, 135
Keil, Petr, **182**
Kelley, Edward, *11*
Kerel, Jan, **187**
Kerhart, František, 135
Kerhart, Vojtěch, 135
Kinský, Prince/Count Rudolf, 42, 49
Kinský Villa and Gardens (1827–31), **49**
Kittrich, Josef (1901–68), **158**
Klár, Professor Alois, 50
Klár Institute for the Blind (1836–44), **50**
Klášter a kostel sv. Markéty (1708–45), **34**
Klausen Synagogue, 6
Koch, Heinrich, **49**
Kohl, J. F., 11
Kolátor, Václav, **133**
Koospol Foreign Trade Association building (1974–77), **176**
Koruna Palace (1912–14), **99**
Kostel Nejsvětějšího Srdce Páně (1928–32), **134**
Kostel Panny Marie pod řetězem (1370s), **14**

139

Index

Index

Map A Central Prague

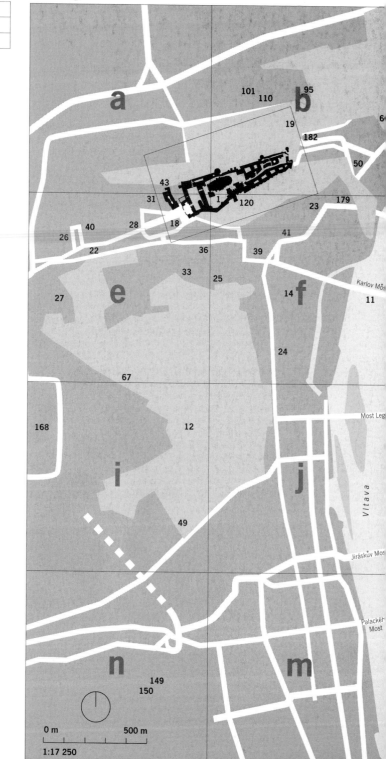

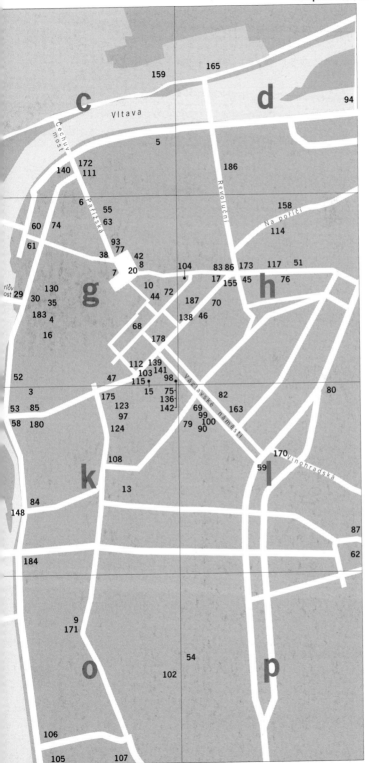

Vltava

Čechův most

159
165
94

c
d

5

186

140 172
111

6 Pařížská
55
63

60 74

61

93 77
38
42
7 20 8

104

83 86 173 117 51
17 155 45 76

10
44 72

187 70

138 46

68

178

112 139
103 141
47 115 98
175 15 75
136
142
123 69
97 99 100
124 79 90

82

163

80

108

k

13

84

148

184

170 Vinohradská
59 l

87

62

9
171

54

o

102

p

106

105 107

rlův
ost 29

130
30 35
183 4
16

52

3
53 85
58 180

g

h

Na poříčí
158
114

Revoluční

Václavské náměstí

Map B Outer Prague

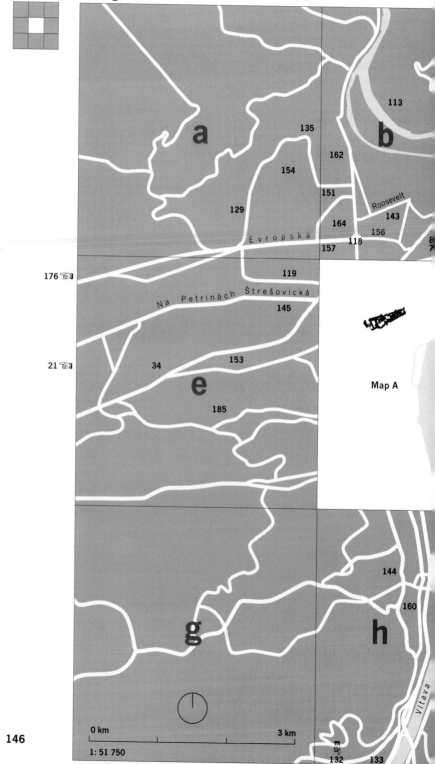

a

135

162

113

b

154

151

Roosevelt

129

164

143

156

Evropská

118

8
7

157

176

119

Na Petrinách Štrešovická

145

21

34

153

e

Map A

185

g

144

h

160

Vltava

0 km

3 km

1: 51 750

132

133

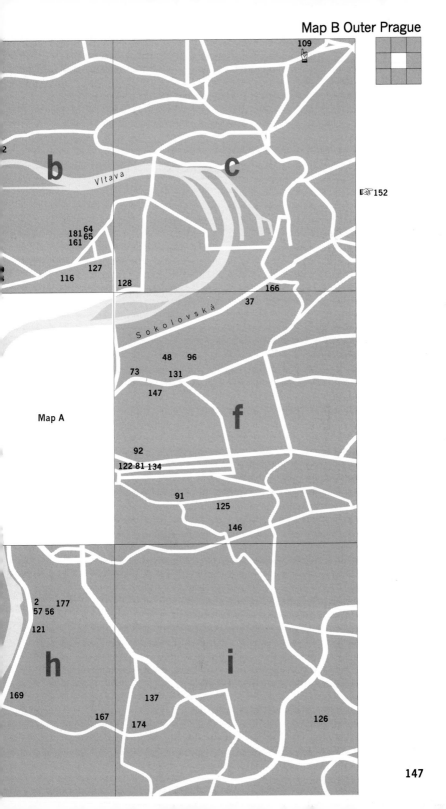

109

☞152

b

Vltava

c

181 64
65
161

127

116

128

166

37

Sokolovská

48   96

73   131

147

f

92

122 81 134

91

125

146

Map A

2   177
57 56

121

h

i

169

137

167   174

126